20 ICONS OF SIERRA LEONE

WHO SHAPED HISTORY

CURATED BY AKINDELE T.M. DECKER & ADRIAN Q. LABOR

ILLUSTRATED BY SAMANTHA EVERETTE

20 ICONS OF SIERRA LEONE

WHO SHAPED HISTORY

CURATED BY AKINDELE T.M. DECKER & ADRIAN Q. LABOR

ILLUSTRATED BY SAMANTHA EVERETTE

FIRST EDITION

www.africancurator.com

TABLE OF CONTENTS

ACKNOWLEDGEMENTS

Sierra Leone is well positioned historically as a place of value for students of modern history. Since the middle-ages, it has served major roles in shaping history, particularly during the trans-atlantic slave trade and post-slavery. It was a key place in Africa where the ideological fight to dismantle colonization developed. The contributions of its people, evolving from a tapestry of Africa and the African Diaspora, helped to usher in pan-africanism and subsequently the call for independence. History will eventually highlight its continued role in Africa as the continent comes of age in this modern technology era.

Efforts have been made before to compile lists of Sierra Leonean Heroes. For the last 50+ years, much of the same set of Heroes have been celebrated. With its rich history and heritage, it is important that as many of its historical icons are known, especially by young generations of Sierra Leoneans. Promoting this effort in a series of Icon compilations, curated through in-depth research and emerging technology is a core goal of African Curator. Our primary goal for the Sierra Leone Icon series is to increase awareness among all Sierra Leoneans about people who helped shape the history of Sierra Leone and around the world.

This first step to draw a silver lining from the first recorded accounts of Sierra Leone, its people and its lands, through several centuries would not be possible without those who wrote the accounts. These include those who wrote the newspapers; the historians who compiled the accounts across time and those who published their stories or their communities' stories. We are thankful for them. This book is a modern day approach to highlight the many historic milestones made by ordinary Sierra Leoneans who grew to be icons in their own right. Curating the history of these icons involved researching literature as well as accounts from primary sources. The process left us, the authors, enlightened about inspiring Sierra Leoneans and their uncelebrated contributions and achievements at home and abroad. We have done our best to balance facts, the emotions and the illustrations to deliver a book that will inspire a wide range of young adults about Sierra Leone. A land that we will eventually learn to love regardless of the highs and lows.

We, Akindele and Adrian, are thankful for the support of our wives, Nanah Decker and Bidemi Carrol respectively and our children. Adrian is grateful for the push from his daughters Thandi, Dominique and Mahogany to see this project through. Another notable encouragement for Adrian to take on this project was the many enlightened and inspiring moments, over the years, that he got from Dr. Ismail Rashid's accounts of Sierra Leone through his historic lens. Akindele's extensive activities in promoting Sierra Leone's culture and history over the years in numerous local, national and diaspora organizations created the foundation for this initiative. We are grateful for friends and colleagues who gave time to help through the editing of the book. They include; Samuel Mahoi; Fatmata Jalloh, Emma Pyne-Bailey, Fara Jawara, Wilma Jones, Ph.D., Geoffrey Thomas, Hannah Kallon, Barbara Morgan, Rosamarie Jah, George Lewis, Jose Paulissen-Dougan, Manje Kargbo, Danna Labor, Connie Kargbo, Arthur Burney-Nicol, Dr. Alusine Jalloh, Lucilda Hunter, Honourable Paramount Chief Masa Paki Kebombor II, Abdul Karim Turay, and Aminata Jalloh.

SIERRA LEONE, WEST AFRICA

Sierra Leone is located in the western part of Africa. It has a population of almost 8 million people. Its about 27,00 square miles or 71,000 sq km. It was divided into 14 Districts before 2017 and now has 16 Districts, including Karene and Falaba.

DR. ARTHUR ABRAHAM

1945 - 2020

Professor Arthur Abraham, son of the soil, was a university historian who spent his career understanding and recounting Sierra Leone's history from an internal viewpoint as far back as the 1500s. Arthur Abraham was born on July 12, 1945 in Daru Town in Kailahun district, and interestingly he died on his birthday 75 years later on July 12, 2020 in Freetown. He grew up in the colonial era when Sierra Leone was a country with two parts. One part was a colony covering present day Western Area since 1808 and the other part was a protectorate comprising the present-day provincial districts since 1896. The history of Sierra Leone was centred mainly on European involvement in the continent and few scholarly works explained the different ethnic groups that are now part of a national construct. Professor Abraham made it his life's work and has left numerous intellectual trails for other scholars to follow up on.

Professor Arthur Abraham received his Bachelor (honours) from Durham University in 1967, his Master of Arts from University of Sierra Leone in 1971 and his Doctor of Philosophy from Birmingham University U.K. in 1974. Professor Abraham advanced his career through his roles as a lecturer, senior lecturer, professor and Dean at the University of Sierra Leone between 1973-1997. During this period, he also held an associate professorship at Cuttington University College, Liberia between 1978-1980. Professor Abraham was a visiting professor at Long Island University, New York between 1997- 1999. Thereafter he emigrated to the US and became a Professor at Virginia State University until his retirement. Upon retirement he returned home and was appointed as Pro-Chancellor of Njala University in 2020.

1400

Ethnographic studies have shown that the ethnic groups Sherbro-bullom, Temne, Loko, Limbas, Krim and Gola occupied present day Sierra Leone in 1400s.

1462

Serra Lyoa was the name recorded by Portuguese explorer Pedro Da Sintra to describe the Sierra Leone coast. He explained that Serra meant Mountains and Lyoa, the rough land.

Professor Arthur Abraham was a first-generation university historian unearthing Sierra Leone's history. While a student, he laid out the foundation of one of his life's work in his master's dissertation about traditional systems of governance, "The Rise of Traditional Leadership among the Mende: A Study in the Acquisition of Political Power." This allowed him to look back and challenge the Eurocentric history of Sierra Leone and advance the more significant impact of West Africa's ancient empires (Ghana, Mali and Songhai) as well as the Mani Invasions on the ethnic landscape of the country. Thereafter in his PhD dissertation, "Mende Government and Politics Under Colonial Rule: Historical Study of Sierra Leone, 1890-1937" he attempted to explain the interplay of traditional governance and colonial rule. In 1977, he shared his intellectual opinion at the colloquium during the pan african cultural events.

"WHILE THE CULTURAL AND HISTORICAL STUDIES ON SIERRA LEONE ARE IN NO SENSE STATIC, THEIR PROGRESS IS SLOW."

Professor Abraham was instrumental in the setting up of the Historical Society of Sierra Leone, headed by George Anthony at Milton Margai Teachers College (MMTC). He was elected as the editor-in-chief of the Journal of the Society. A graduate of Professor Abraham remarked that by the late 1970s, the professor was undoubtedly the most published in the department. He lamented that the Professor should have been made Head of the History Department of University of Sierra Leone at a crucial time when direction was needed.

In one of his more recent papers, re-examining cultural policy in Sierra Leone, Professor Abraham spoke of the pros and cons of the prevailing cultural perspective and the unanswered questions of the "Nomoli" in our distant past. He concluded that while cultural and historical studies in Sierra Leone are in no sense static, their progress is slow. He signaled that more historical evidence remains to be unearthed by archaeology work in Sierra Leone.

1500

The Kissi migrated south west into Sierra Leone due to a Koranko invasion from the north. The kissi occupied a region that cuts across the borders of Sierra Leone, Guinea and Liberia.

1508

Manguy (mange) was the largest town of some thousand persons that was recorded for Serra Lyoa. Portuguese trader, Alvaro Velho, livin in Serra Lyoa, recorded that the inhabitants called their country Pymto after a village in the Mountains.

During his tenure at the Virginia State University, he acted as consultant to two Hollywood movies. This helped shaped public and popular perception of how the historical events around the La Amistad Revolt (1998) and Blood Diamonds (2005) are perceived today.

Professor Abraham's last book, "An Introduction to the Pre-Colonial History of the Mende of Sierra Leone", published in 2003, lays many trails for future historians to follow and intervene in the ethnogenesis discussion of the people of Sierra Leone. In his wisdom, as a university historian on Sierra Leone and as the grandfather of the nation's ethnic history, he points all towards the dispersal of Mande culture and the spread of Mende as a lingua franca.

NOMOLI, SOAPSTONE FIGURINES, ARE NOW REGARDED AS SOME OF THE EARLIEST WORKS OF ART FROM SIERRA LEONE. THESE FAMOUS SOAPSTONE FIGURINES ARE FOUND BURIED IN FOOTPATHS, RIVERBANKS, IN FORESTS AND MOUNTAIN TOPS OVER VAST AREAS OF THE HINTERLAND. THEY STILL POSE AN ENIGMA. HISTORIANS STILL HAVE THE CHALLENGE TO ANSWER THESE QUESTIONS ABOUT THE NOMOLI LEFT UNANSWERED BY ARTHUR ABRAHAM. WHO CARVED THEM? WHEN? WHAT PURPOSE DID THEY SERVE THEN AS DISTINCT FROM THEIR RITUAL USES TODAY?. HE HAS SUGGESTED THAT THE CREATION OF THE NOMOLIS ARE ATTRIBUTED TO THE COASTAL CULTURES IN THE MID-SIXTEENTH CENTURY AND WERE LEFT BEHIND AS THE MANI INVASIONS OF THOSE TIMES FORCED PEOPLE TO ABANDON VILLAGES AND TOWNS. TODAY THESE FIGURINES ARE KNOWN AS NOMOLI BY COASTAL AND SOME INTERIOR ETHNIC GROUPS AND PUEDMO/PUEDMA BY THE KISSI PEOPLE. MANY ETHNIC GROUPS BURY THEM IN THE THEIR FARM AS THEY BELIEVE THE NOMOLI FIGURES WILL GIVE THEM HEALTH AND GOOD HARVEST. THE KISSI PEOPLE USE THEM IN SHRINES AND AS PART OF THEIR BELIEF THAT ANCESTRAL SPIRITS ACT AS MEDIATORS BETWEEN THE COMMUNITY AND GOD.
~ PROFESSOR ARTHUR ABRAHAM

1567

The first Mani (Manneh or Mane) invasion of Serra Lyoa resulted in Mani's settling in Temne and Bullom lands. The Susu, the Fulani, the Yalunka, the Loko and the Limba repelled and stood their ground against the Mani.

1800

The Kono, the Vias, the Yalunkas, the Korankos and the Mende nations entered present day Sierra Leone between 1600-1800 as a result of different invasions.

JOHN AKAR

1927 - 1975

John Joseph Akar was born on May 20,1927 in Rotifunk, the central town in Bompeh chiefdom of Moyamba District. Bompeh Chiefdom has an estimated 207 villages with the bompeh river cutting across its land on route to the Yawri bay by the Atlantic Ocean. John Akar's mother was Sherbro and his father was Lebanase. At home, in Rotifunk, he attended the Evangelical United Brethren Church primary school and then went on to the Albert Academy secondary school in Freetown. In 1947, he left Sierra Leone to study Radio and Television at Otterbein College, Ohio, USA and obtained a Bachelor of Arts degree from the University of California at Berkeley. Thereafter he pursued his postgraduate studies in England at Lincoln's Inn at the London school of Economics. John Akar returned home to Sierra Leone in 1957 and began an extraordinary career as an artist, composer, broadcaster and producer.

During his training abroad, he evolved his expertise as a broadcaster, short storywriter, actor, playwright, poet and journalist, while he appeared on the London and New York stages. His notable plays are "Cry tamba" , "The valley without echo" and "Encounter." Akar worked as a freelancer for the British Broadcasting Company from 1950 to 1955, the Voice of America, 1955 to 1956 and the worldwide broadcasting system in New York from 1956 to 1957. In his BBC broadcasting program in 1954, "Time to go to School", John Akar recounted the happy days of work and play during his childhood in Sierra Leone.

1801

The idea for the first newspaper in the Colony of Freetown was born during a dinner conversation by Sierra Leone Company staff on Janaury 30, 1801. It was called the Sierra Leone Gazette. Briefly renamed African Herald in 1809.

1934

The Sierra Leone Broadcasting Service (SLBS) was formed from the Freetown Rediffusion Service making it the earliest English language radio broadcast service in West Africa.

He performed in several other plays such as "A Time to Be Born" (1953) and "The Queen's Admiral" (1953). On March 29, 1956, in New York, John Akar performed the opening for the lead character Benjamin, in the play "Mister Johnson." It was a story about Benjamin: A childlike West African man who yearns to become a "civilized" British man.

On his return to Sierra Leone in 1957, he was appointed Head of Programs for the Sierra Leone Broadcasting Service (SLBS). Three years later he was promoted to Director of Broadcasting. In 1963, Akar founded the National Dance Troupe to encourage Sierra Leoneans to have pride in their cultural heritage. A year later, the National Dance Troupe performed at New York World's Fair. This brought widespread recognition to the Dance Troupe and they continued to perform worldwide since. Under his direction the Dance Troupe promoted cultural appreciation within the country. In the West African region, the National Dance Troupe were regular participants in landmark black arts, cultural and pan africanism events such as festival FESTAC 66 in Nigeria and FESTAC 77 in Senegal.

"THE FIRST WORLD FESTIVAL OF BLACK ARTS OR WORLD FESTIVAL OF NEGRO ARTS WAS HELD IN DAKAR, SENEGAL, 1-24 APRIL 1966, INITIATED BY FORMER PRESIDENT LEOPOLD SENGHOR, UNDER THE AUSPICES OF UNESCO. 45 AFRICAN, EUROPEAN, AND CARIBBEAN COUNTRIES PARTICIPATED. IT FEATURED BLACK LITERATURE, MUSIC, THEATER, VISUAL ARTS, FILM AND DANCE".

A year before independence from Britain, Mr. Akar composed the music for the National Anthem of Sierra Leone and published the Sierra Leone National Anthem written by Clifford Nelson Fyle in Mende and Temne. In his capacity as Chairman of the Sierra Leone Museum and the Monuments and Relics Commission he promoted history and cultural preservation.

In keeping with his career as a public servant, Mr. Akar took on other official roles and competed for elected offices.

1963

Television broadcasts started in 1963 as a cooperation between SLBS and commercial interests. Construction began on a new Broadcasting House a decade late and it was never completed.

1964

Sierra Leone National Dance Troupe first won widespread acclaim at the New York World's Fair.

He accepted the ambassadorship to the USA and served from July 1969 to March 1971 and thereafter he attempted to run for an elected office in Parliament. His bid for an elected office was unsuccessful as it coincided with the creation of a racially biased citizenship law in Sierra Leone in 1973 that discriminates against persons born in the country of non-negro African parentage.

Regrettably, Mr. Akar resigned from public service when he disapproved of the turn the government was also taking towards a one-party state. In 1973, he left for Jamaica where he became active in broadcasting and journalism. He died two years later in his adopted country and his remains were quietly brought to Rotifunk for burial where he now rests. He has yet to be remembered as an iconic Sierra Leonean deserving of posthumous national recognition.

ONE WITH A FAITH THAT WISDOM INSPIRES,
ONE WITH A ZEAL THAT NEVER TIRES;
EVER WE SEEK TO HONOUR THY NAME,
OURS IS THE LABOUR, THINE THE FAME.
WE PRAY THAT NO HARM ON THY CHILDREN MAY FALL,
THAT BLESSING AND PEACE MAY DESCEND ON US ALL;
SO MAY WE SERVE THEE EVER ALONE,
LAND THAT WE LOVE, OUR SIERRA LEONE.

~

2ND VERSE NATIONAL ANTHEM WRITTEN BY CLIFFORD NELSON FLYE

1966

1st World Festival of Black Arts or World Festival of Negro Arts, in Dakar, Senegal. Sierra Leone participated among 45 African, European, Caribbean countries to feature black literature, music, theater and more.

1977

FESTAC '77, also known as the Second World Festival Black and African Festival of Arts and Culture was a major international festival held in Lagos, Nigeria from mid January to mid February.

ALHAJI MOMODU ALLIE

1800s - 1948

Alhaji Momodu Allie was a Fula Chief, who served the Fula Town community in Freetown from 1931-1948. He holds the longest Fula chieftaincy. He was elected by his community and recognized by the Colonial Government. In this capacity, Alhaji Allie oversaw the growth of the islamic community, Fula Town, in the east of Freetown. He also expanded the trading relationship between Fuuta Jalon and Freetown that began a century earlier.

Alhaji Momodu Allie was originally from hacundemaje region in the Fuuta Jalon mountain. In 1904, he left Fuuta Toro, a region along the Senegal river with cattle to trade. Momodu Allie traveled across to Bathurst in Gambia then south to Conakry in Guinea, and eventually to Freetown. Over the next forty years he raised his family and built his commercial opportunities in the butchering business and in real estate, becoming a successful entrepreneur in colonial Sierra Leone. Allie's efforts laid the foundation for many other Fula families to integrate successfully against challenges to their community during colonial and post-colonial times. Fulas can be found everywhere in Sierra Leone and their ancestors can be traced back to Fuuta Jalon, as they retained their clan identities or jettooje (family names).

He laid the foundation for many other Fula families to integrate successfully against challenges to their community during colonial and post colonial times.

1800

Solima Yalunka state created after the Fuuta Jalon Jihad became the home to the Yalunkas and it covers an area partly in Guinea and partly in the northeastern part of Sierra Leone.

1819

The first settled muslim community at Fula Town in the east end of Freetown comprising Fulas and Mandinkas.

Alusine Jalloh, in his book, "African Entrepreneurship: Muslim Fula Merchants in Sierra Leone", highlighted Alhaji Momodu Allie's operations and wealth as a cattle trade and butcher. Jalloh wrote " he had eighteen warehs in different areas of Freetown such as Calabar town and Hastings during the colonial period. At the height of World War II, Alhaji Allie had as many as eight hundred cows in one wareh alone. Cattle entered Freetown market from the northern province and were trucked from Makeni to Freeown. Those that entered through Kambia were loaded onto launches at Gberie, Kasiri and Rokupr and transported down Sierra Leone river to "Cow Yard", an abattoir on the wharf at Magazine cut in the east end."

In the mid eighteenth century, the Fula leaders launched a series of jihads targeted against the Yalunka people who also inhabited the Fuuta Jalon region. This resulted in the Yalunka people migrating south and the eventual creation of the Solima Yalunka state in present day Guinea and Sierra Leone's northeastern border region in the nineteenth century. The earliest governing administration in Freetown, the Sierra Leone Company (1792- 1815), sent trade delegations to Timbo, the capital of Fuuta Jalon, to meet the Almamy. The subsequent British colonial administration(1815-1961) also recognized the importance of Fula caravan trade and continued to send trade delegations to the Almamy of Fuuta Jalon.

"IN THE 1830S, FODE IBRAHIM TARAWALI, WHO WAS EDUCATED AT TOUBA WAS GRANTED LAND AT GBILE OPPOSITE KAMBIA ON THE KOLENTE RIVER. HE USED IT TO DEVELOP AN IMPORTANT MUSLIM CENTRE FOR HIGHER EDUCATION AND IT FLOURISHED UNTIL 1870S."

Alhaji Momodu Allie later invested in urban real estate properties and owned various types of properties, primarily single shops and multiple storey houses with ground floor shops. He had rental rooming houses that adjoined family houses scattered throughout the city.

In his time, Islamic education of children was favored and western education was opposed. Western education was thought of as a first step to Christain conversion that could result in the children pursuing non-trading professions which conflicted with Alhaji Momodu Allie's goals of maintaining the family business. His sons inherited his business and did indeed go on to build on his success in real estate.

1840

Lantern Parade began when Muslims in the Liberated African community of Fourah bay and Fula Town marched in procession from the east of Freetown to the Government house as the concluding celebration of Ramadan.

1901

The Governor appointed Dr E. W. Blyden as Director of Mohammedan Education and the Mohammedan Education Ordinance was adopted a year later.

In 1905 the British governor introduced Ordinance 19 titled "An ordinance to promote a system of Administration by Tribal Authority among tribes settled in Freetown". It recognized and empowered Chiefs, Alimamies and Headmen in the city across all groups.

On the death of Fula Chief Alimamy Jambura In 1931, Alle Momodou was put forward to act as Alimamy on account of him having been an assistant to an earlier Almamy from Fuuta Toro between 1912-1918. Following an election in 1933, the colonial administration recognized Alhaji Momodu Allie as permanent chief. He held this chief title even after re-elections were called based on petitions filed in three different years by his opponents.

Following his death in 1948, there was a break in Fula chieftaincy politics until 1956. Interestingly the Fula families vying for power and the recognition that comes with it, traded among each other, and avoided chieftaincy politics from ruining their businesses.

"FODE IBRAHIM TARAWALI, WHO WAS EDUCATED AT TOUBA WAS GRANTED LAND AT GBILE OPPOSITE KAMBIA ON THE KOLENTE RIVER IN THE 1830S. HE USED IT TO DEVELOP AN IMPORTANT MUSLIM CENTRE FOR HIGHER EDUCATION AND IT FLOURISHED UNTIL 1870S. PROFESSOR E. W. BLYDEN VISITED GBILE IN JANAURY OF 1872 AND DESCRIBED A MUSLIM UNIVERSITY UNDER THE DIRECTION OF FODE TARAWALI AND HIS SONS. THIS EDUCATIONAL INSTITUTION HAD ABOUT 500 STUDENTS WHO WERE STUDYING VARIOUS ISLAMIC SCIENCES AND DURING THE FORTY YEARS OF ITS EXISTENCE MANY PROMINENT POLITICAL AND RELIGIOUS LEADERS WERE TRAINED THERE. FODE TARAWALI WAS REFERRED TO AS THE HIGH PRIEST OF MORIAH BY COLONIAL OFFICIALS. HE MEDIATED NUMEROUS CONFLICTS BETWEEN THE SUSU AND TEMNE FORCES." ~ DAVID SKINNER

1927
Fuuta Jalon Jihad contributed to the emigration of Fula scholars, clerics, traders, and herdsmen into Freetown and the Protectorate of Sierra Leone.

1932
Formation of Sierra Leone Muslim congress was to build on earlier efforts of the Muhammadan Education Board to unify Muslims and promote Islamic education.

MADAM HONORIA BAILOR-CAULKER

1923 - 1999

Honoria Remmie was born on May 15, 1923 and grew up in the Sherbro community of Kargboro Chiefdom in Moyamba District. Honoria Remmie graduated from the Harford School for Girls, which has educated many women leaders. She was one of the first women to be trained as a teacher at the Fourah Bay College. Honoria began her life of service as a school teacher at the Evangelical United Brethren Missionary School. She met and married A. Max Bailor, a school teacher who later became the headmaster. Honoria Bailor-Caulker went on to become the Paramount Chief of Kargboro Chiefdom before her 39th birthday.

On Sunday May 6, 1962 Honoria Bailor-Caulker was installed as Paramount Chief of Kargboro Chiefdom. Her election the year before on December 18, 1961 was unprecedented in Kargboro as she competed against three women and seven men for the title, to rule over 23,000 people in a chiefdom of about 22 square miles.

The 304 all-male chiefdom councilors elected Madam Honoria Bailor-Caulker as Paramount Chief. On the day of her installation, hundreds of people traveled from towns and villages in Kargboro and the neighboring chiefdoms, to the town of Shenge on the Atlantic coast, to attend the formal ceremony and dedication service for the new Paramount Chief.

1819

Waterloo Village, originally called Ma Porto, was resettled in 1819 by soldiers from the second and fourth West India Regiment from Jamaica and Barbados who returned from the Battle of Waterloo in present-day Belgium where Napoleon Bornaparte was defeated.

1820

Banana Island was ceded on October 20 to the Colonial Government of Sierra Leone by Thomas Kon Tham and George Stephen Caulker.

Paramount Chief Honoria Bailor-Caulker was a strong advocate for Women's issues. She became the first Sierra Leone conference president of the Women's Society of World Service. At the 1977 American Anthropological Association meeting on women in government and politics, she gave a memorable speech as a guest speaker. She began by singing the hymn Amazing Grace, and went on to explain how the words to the well-known song written by Methodist preacher John Newton, reflect repentance for his actions as a former slave trader in Sherbro land. In her speech, Honoria acknowledged the Sherbro people's participation along with British and American traders, in the enslavement of Africans. She went on to represent the Sierra Leone government at the Fourth World Conference on Women in Beijing China.

> "THE SHERBRO PEOPLE LIVE MUCH IN THE PATRIARCHAL WAY. AN OLD MAN USUALLY PRESIDES IN EACH TOWN, WHOSE AUTHORITY DEPENDS MORE ON HIS YEARS THAN ON HIS POSSESSIONS: AND HE WHO IS CALLED THE KING, IS NOT EASILY DISTINGUISHED, EITHER BY STATE OR WEALTH, FROM ALL THE REST. BUT THE DIFFERENT DISTRICTS, WHICH SEEM TO BE, IN MANY RESPECTS, INDEPENDENT OF EACH OTHER ARE INCORPORATED AND UNITED , BY MEANS OF AN INSTITUTION WHICH PERVADES THEM ALL, AND IT IS CALLED THE PUUROW (PORO). JOHN NEWTON, 1788"

In her chiefdom, Honoria Bailor-Caulker encouraged communal work and fishing cooperatives. Under her direction, the International Labor Organization paved the road from Moyamba to Shenge, an important thoroughfare. On her initiative, the Fisheries Department established a facility in Shenge. Madam Bailor-Caulker started the Howard Memorial secondary school in 1967. She regularly visited the 11 sections of Kargboro Chiefdom under her rule. Her speaker and town crier would use a horn blower to announce her arrival. Dancers, singers, and drummers would meet her and carry her in a hammock to the section's court barray, where they would hear her speak and address issues of concern.

1849

On Tasso Island, the Caulker ruling family's homestead, a treaty was signed to end the Sherbro Caulker family wars and establish the extent of the Kargboro chiefdom, Bompeh Chiefdom and Ribbi chiefdom.

1890

Madam Yoko, "Queen of Senehun", gave land to establish a new school for girls in Moyamba. The school was completed in two years and named Harford School after Mrs Lillian R. Harford, an American organizer, author, and president of the Women's Missionary Association.

In November 1995, during the civil war, she left shenge for Freetown for her safety. While in Freetown, she had an accidental fall in an open excavation on the street and broke her hip. She was admitted to the Military Forces hospital on March 24, 1997 at Wilberforce. Her condition worsened amidst wartime restrictions which delayed her trip to the USA for surgery that had been organized by family and missionary friends.

On arrival she was too frail to undergo surgery and later died in Silver Spring, Maryland on April 27, 1999. Her body was taken to Sierra Leone and buried beside her grandmother at the Gomer Memorial Church in Shenge. Her grandmother was Sophia Neale Caulker (1898-1909), the granddaughter of George Stephen Caulker I (1810 -1831), both former Paramount Chiefs of Kargboro Chiefdom.

ECONOMIC DEVELOPMENT WAS SPURRED BY THE RAPID COMPLETION IN 1908 OF THE RAILROAD TO PENDEMBU ON THE COUNTRY'S EASTERN FRINGE. IT WAS A SLOW, NARROW-GAUGE LINE THAT NEVER SUCCEEDED IN RUNNING AT A PROFIT. NEVERTHELESS ITS CONSTRUCTION, COINCIDING WITH THE FINAL ENDING OF INTERTRIBAL WARFARE, LED TO ALMOST IMMEDIATE REORGANIZATION OF THE ECONOMY. IT PROVIDED A ROUTE FOR HIGH-VOLUME PRODUCE, PALM NUTS, KOLA NUTS, RUBBER, AND RICE, WHICH THE INTERIOR HAD BEEN CAPABLE OF PRODUCING BUT COULD NOT EARLIER MOVE TO MARKETS EXCEPT AS HEADLOADS ALONG NARROW TRAILS. BETWEEN THE END OF THE HUT TAX WAR AND 1912, EXPORTS HAD TRIPLED AND THE GOVERNMENT'S REVENUE FROM CUSTOMS TAXES HAD GONE UP EVEN MORE. PALM OIL AND KOLA NUTS WERE THE MAINSTAYS OF THE COUNTRY'S ECONOMY, AND THE INCOME FROM THEIR SALE WENT LARGELY TO LOCAL SMALL-HOLDERS SINCE NO PLANTATIONS EXISTED.

1898

The Hut Tax war began with resistance by Bai bureh's warrior to the British colonial forces' attempt to arrest him at Kasseh. Protectorate chiefs, opposed the imposition of 5 shilling per house in the protectorate since 2 years prior.

1907

The corner foundations were laid for the Berry street campus of Albert Academy, in Freetown. The secondary school for boys was opened a year later and named in memory of Dr. Ira D. Albert, a missionary at Shenge.

BAI
BUREH
1840s - 1908

Bai Bureh was born near Makeni, Bombali District in the Northern Province of Sierra Leone. He is believed by some, to be of Temne and Loko origin. Kebalai, as he was called in his younger days, grew up as a warrior, known for his brave and courageous spirit. His father sent him to Gbendembu Ngowahun to develop his warrior character. He became a very useful soldier and leader to several chiefs in the region such as a local chief called Bokarie. By the 1880s, he had earned himself great reputation as a skilled fighter and leader.

In 1887, he was chosen by Temne elders of Kasseh Chiefdom to become ruler of Kasseh. It was then that he took on the name, Bai Bureh. He wasted no time in proving his worth by helping local leaders secure sovereignty and further their causes by protecting their interests.

In 1890, Bai Bureh helped a leader called Karimu in a battle against the Limba. It was one of the moments were he demonstrated his tendency to be outspoken about his beliefs and expectations for the principles he honored. He openly exhibited his distaste for the conduct of peace talks between the Limba and Loko following the battle, particularly because he was wilfully left out of the deliberations leading to the treaty.

1500s
A major trading center known by some as Os Alagoas is renamed Port Logo. By 1821, the standard spelling had become Port Loko.

1780s
A Loko named Gumbu Smart is enslaved at Bunce Island. Because of his intelligence, he gained his freedom and became one of the most powerful chiefs in the region.

Around 1891, Bai Bureh and about 1,500 of his troops fought alongside the colonial British troops against a local rival. He also helped the 1st West Indian Regiment attack a local leader called Tambi. Bai Bureh proved reliable to regional chiefs as well as the colonial administration.

In 1896, the hinterland of Sierra Leone around the Freetown Colony was officially designated the Sierra Leone Protectorate. Treaties were signed with local chiefs outlining the terms for designation as a Protectorate. By 1898, one of these terms included a hut tax imposed by the British colonial administration. The imposed tax was based on the size of a Protectorate resident's hut. Many local chiefs and residents in the Protectorate opposed the tax, which they felt was unnjust and unfairly imposed. Many Freetown residents, particularly local newspapers also publicly critized the timing and enforcement of the tax.

"IN 1896, THE SIERRA LEONE PROTECTORATE WAS DECLARED AND BY 1898, A HOUSE (HUT) TAX WAS IMPOSED. BAI BUREH LED A CROSS-SECTION OF RESISTANCE AGAINST THE HUT TAX AND FOR MONTHS, FIGHTING OCCURRED. HE WAS CONSIDERED THE COLONIAL GOVERNMENT'S PRINCIPAL OPPONENT TO PAYING THE HUT TAX AND BAI BUREH CONSISTENTLY ESCAPED SEVERAL ATTEMPTS BY COLONIAL TROOPS TO CAPTURE HIM."

As the Colonial Government went from town to town to collect the tax, many chiefs refused to pay, while others leaned favorably towards paying the tax. Bai Bureh, already known for his outspokeness against issues dear to him, refused to pay. When the British attempted to force him, he revolted, and was a fierce opponent in the battles that followed. Bai Bureh proved himself a courageous military strategist. For months, the British troops tried repeatedly to capture Bai Bureh and end his uprising, but they were usually unsuccessful. Other chiefs in the area also followed course in resisting the demand by the Colonial Government to pay the Hut Tax, such as Bai Kompa and Sena Bundu. Other regional chiefs such as Nancy Tucker, Madam Yoko, and others continued to pay their taxes to the British.

1787

Treaty signed between British and Temne Chiefs for land in western Sierra Leone. It was settled by about 400 black settlers from England and America called the Black Poor.

1791

The Temne King, Naimbana, sent his son, Prince John Frederic Naimbana to school in England. He was a great student, though he died on his voyage back to Sierra Leone in 1793.

For about 10 months, Bai Bureh held a fierce resistance to the colonial tax policy. Another uprising, seemingly against the Hut tax, also took place around the same time in the Mende regions. Throughout towns such as Rotifunk, Taiama, Yele, Bonthe, Sembehun, and Gallinas towns, many people were killed by local militias. Many targeted victims included those considered non-natives, such as Creoles and foreign Missionaries. In Freetown, a local militia was formed to defend the city against possible attacks. The Freetown Mayor, James Taylor, and Dr. Renner were two of the few residents who joined. Leaders such as Kai Kai, defended Bandajuma from the uprising, while Momo Ja and others helped to defend Gallinas towns.

After much efforts by colonial troops, Bai Bureh was arrested and taken prisoner. His imprisonment forced the colonial administration to visit the issue of whether people of the Protectorate were British subjects. He was moved from Karene to Freetown, where he received favorable reactions from some of the residents. Some of them believed that his resistance was not reflective of the other inhumane killings undertaken during the uprisings. His resistance was seen as a legitimate effort to counter an unfair policy. In 1898, Bai Bureh and a few other chiefs involved in the war were deported to the Gold Coast. He returned to Sierra Leone years later and resumed his title again in 1905 until his death in 1908.

THE CHALMERS REPORT WAS PREPARED IN 1899 BY A SCOTTISH COMMISSIONER CALLED SIR DAVID CHALMERS. IT WAS AN EFFORT TO PROVIDE AN ACCOUNT OF ALL THAT TOOK PLACE DURING THE HUT TAX WAR, BASED ON TESTIMONIES AND OTHER EVIDENCES. ACCORDING TO THE REPORT, IT WAS FOUND THAT THE HUT TAX POLICY AND METHODS USED IN COLLECTING IT, PLAYED A MAJOR ROLE TO INFLAME THE UPRISINGS IN THE PROTECTORATE. MANY TO-DATE HAVE REFERENCED THE REPORT AS AN EXONERATION OF BAI BUREH. DISTINCTIONS HAVE ALSO BEEN MADE BETWEEN THE TEMNE AND MENDE UPRISINGS, IN THE CAUSES AND DESTRUCTIONS THAT RESULTED FROM EACH. MANY SCHOLARS HAVE NOTED THAT THE MENDE UPRISINGS WHICH RESULTED IN THE DEATH OF MANY INNOCENT VICTIMS, WAS NOT DIRECTLY LINKED TO BAI BUREH'S REVOLT.

1796

"Quit-rent" levy was imposed on lands owned by Freetown's black settlers by the British owned Sierra Leone Company. It met great resistance from the settlers which ultimately led to a revolt in 1800.

1815

Temne recover Port Loko from the Susu. They fought the Loko for another 20 years, between 1820s and 1840s.

MIRANDA OLAYINKA BURNEY-NICOL

1927 - 1996

Miranda Olayinka Burney-Nicol was born in Freetown, in 1927. Her father, Arthur Burney-Nicol was a government medical dispenser and her mother, Phyllis, was a trader. She entered Annie Walsh Memorial School in 1932. In the early 1940s, she taught briefly at the Harford School for Girls in Moyamba District.

Olayinka, as she was commonly called, traveled to New York in the late 1940s with a scholarship opportunity to further her studies in the arts. She delved into a variety of art disciplines including painting, textile, murals, and sculpting. She spent several years at Long Island University in New York and Ball State Teachers' College in Indiana. She continued her studies in London in 1954, studying murals and oil paintings across Europe. She attended the Central School of Arts and Crafts in London. She also spent a year in France working with textiles.

Olayinka returned to Sierra Leone in 1958 at age 31. Independence from colonial Britain was finally taking shape. Nationalism was a central aim for all and many artists and writers played a contributing role to ensure that the nation achieved it. Artists such as Hassan Bangurah were employed by the Sierra Leone Broadcasting Service and other governmental agencies.

1490

Ivory carvings have been discovered in Sierra Leone by Archeologists and others. They are believed to have been crafted between 1490 and 1530, by inhabitants of the Sierra Leone region.

1861

Big Market in Freetown was built by Afro-West Indian, Charles Hazelborg. It is now one of the National Monuments of Sierra Leone. The market today serves as a marketplace for local arts and crafts artisans.

Olayinka was offered the position of Government Artist by the Ministry of Education, which she held for about 10 years. As Government Artist during Independence celebrations, she was responsible for coordinating visual arts across the country. Murals were created on several buildings in Freetown that illustrated the dynamic and rich cultural heritage and history of Sierra Leone. Artists of the time, such as Hassan Bangurah and John Vandi brought in creative inspiration from other provinces in Sierra Leone. Others such as Louise Metzger and Rosemarie Marke helped to lay a foundation for the modern artist profession in Sierra Leone through their work.

According to Author Simon Ottenberg, Olayinka's role as Government Artist, encouraged the integration of arts and crafts into school curriculum across the country. Some of her work also involved integrating a focus on the arts in government programs. According to Historian Arthur Abraham, an Arts Education Division was established in 1974. The division was responsible for developing cultural education and curriculum materials for educators. One of its programs included the Arts Education Association of Sierra Leone.

"THE WESTERNER IS WILLING TO PROMOTE, BUT YOU MUST REGISTER IN HIS APPROVED SCHOOLS, AND YOU MUST BE "PRIMITIVE" OR "NAIVE." IF SHE SAYS SHE IS NO PUPPET, THEN SHE STARVES UNTIL SHE BEHAVES....THUS THE FIGHT IS ON. TO WIN IS TO ENDURE. TO WIN IS MIND OVER MATTER, DECOLONIZING THE SPIRIT, AND ACQUIRING A NEW BORN INDEPENDENCE FROM SLAVERY - MENTAL AND SPIRITUAL SLAVERY." ~ OLAYINKA BURNEY-NICOL AT THE UNITAR 1980 SEMINAR ON CREATIVE WOMEN

Olayinka was very versatile with her art. She developed a reputation as a cultural nationalist, particularly through the cultural diversity of Sierra Leone illustrated in her artwork. In 1964, she designed costumes for the Sierra Leone National Dance Troupe's world tour. Her work often blended African and Western culture and creative expressions. She was known for several artwork of Mende masquerades, such as her oil painting Goboi Dancer in 1972, which was showcased at the Empire and Commonwealth Museum, in Bristol.

1885

An Industrial exhibit was held at Big Market in Freetown. Among the presentations were artwork by ABC Sibthorpe, which included paintings, sculptures, and artificial fruits.

1886

Sierra Leone participated in the Colonial and Indian Exhibition held in England. Exhibitors showcased various artifacts illustrating the culture and heritage of Sierra Leoneans.

Throughout her art career, Olayinka had been inspired by the work of other African women artists. In 1980, she attended a seminar on creative women in changing societies, sponsored by the United Nations Institute of Training and Research. She talked about her experience as a creative female artist from Sierra Leone. Olayinka viewed creative women in Africa as being held between traditional and transitional creative spaces. She also believed creative women also found themselves in both colonial and independent conflicting worlds. She illustrated the colonial struggle of the African creative at that time, creating for a western audience that aimed to guide and guard it. To an African audience, the creative's gifts are viewed as compensation for lesser brain power. It was difficult, based on her experience, for an African creative woman to be both creative and independent in a colonial world.

In 1988, Olayinka traveled to London in her early 60s to continue pursuing art. She passed away in 1996. Olayinka's work has been showcased around the world. In Freetown, she held a solo exhibit in the 1980s at the Mammy Yoko Hotel. in Germany, her work was displayed at the German Parliamentary Society and the Federation of German Industries in Cologne.

SIERRA LEONE'S INDEPENDENCE ERA WAS USHERED IN WITH AN ARTISTIC REVIVAL FROM VARIOUS DISCIPLINES. PLAYWRIGHTS, POETS, WRITERS, ARTISTS, MUSICIANS AND OTHERS EXPRESSED THROUGH THEIR WORKS, THE ESSENCE OF SIERRA LEONEAN NATIONALISM ACROSS THE COUNTRY. THEATRE PRODUCTIONS, ART EXHIBITS, AND MUSIC WERE WRITTEN BY AND FOR SIERRA LEONEANS IN LOCAL LANGUAGES THEY COULD UNDERSTAND AND CONTEXTS THEY COULD RELATE TO.

1977
A Festival Secretariat coordinated the participation of Sierra Leone in the World Black and African Festival of Arts and Culture. A tour across the country recruited talent to join the festival, which was held in Nigeria.

2019
African American, Nakia Wigfall and a local craftswoman made a Shukublai basket in the village of Rogbonko. It was a historic symbolic gesture of the connection between Sierra Leone and African American Gullah people.

ADELAIDE
CASELY-HAYFORD
1868 - 1960

Adelaide Smith Casely-Hayford was born in Freetown in 1868. She was the daughter of William Smith Jr. and Anne Spilsbury Smith. Her maternal Great-grandfather was Thomas Carew, a recaptive butcher who had been liberated from a slave ship in the early 1800s and sent to Freetown. Thomas Carew was a Bambara recaptive and his wife, Betsy, Adelaide's Great-Grandmother was a Hausa trader. Adelaide's father was the Registrar of the Mixed Commission Court, which was responsible for the trials for seized slave ships after 1807.

Many of Adelaide's siblings were pioneers in their professions. Her brother, Dr. Robert Smith, was one of the first Medical Doctors from Sierra Leone and had served as Assistant Colonial Surgeon. Her brother Francis, in 1871, was one of the first Sierra Leoneans to qualify as a Lawyer.

In her younger years, Adelaide studied in England and Germany. She received her Junior Certificate from Jersey Ladies' College at age fourteen. She returned to Freetown in 1892 and started out as a teacher at the Wesleyan Female Institution.

Adelaide founded Girl's Vocational School around 1898, one of the first private secondary schools for girls in Sierra Leone. There had been previous calls for establishing vocational schools in Sierra Leone, Adelaide noticed that vocational schools for girls had not been given much attention. She started her school with about 15 African girls.

1792
Catherine Abernathy, one of the Black Loyalist Settlers from America, served as Schoolmistress at a school for black children in Nova Scotia a decade earlier. She did the same after settling in Freetown in 1792.

1800
About 550 Jamaican Maroons settled in Freetown, from Trelawney Town in Jamaica. They quickly became an industrious group in Freetown.

In 1903, Adelaide married Joseph Casely-Hayford, a Gold Coast Lawyer and Journalist. Joseph Casely-Hayford is best known for forming one of the first nationalist movements in West Africa, the National Congress of British West Africa.

Adelaide and her family lived in the Gold Coast for several years until her return again to Sierra Leone around 1914. She took up teaching music at the Annie Walsh Memorial School. The following year, Adelaide gave a notable address at Wesley Church to residents, titled "The Rights of Women and Christian Marriage". She continued addressing issues related to developing opportunities for technical education for girls. She held several public meetings at the Wilberforce Memorial Hall such as a meeting with the Ladies Pastoral Aid Association. Patrons for her cause included the Colonial Governor, the Chief Justice and Mayor of Freetown.

"IN AUGUST, 1922, ADELAIDE CASELY-HAYFORD ADDRESSED THE NATIONAL COUNCIL OF NEGRO WOMEN IN RICHMOND, VIRGINIA. SHE MET THE RENOWNED AFRICAN AMERICAN EDUCATOR, MARY MCLEOD BETHUNE. BETHUNE LATER BECAME AN ADVISOR TO U.S. PRESIDENT FRANKLIN ROOSEVELT."

By 1919, Adelaide had become President of the Young Women's Christian Association (YWCA). She also became an active member of the Sierra Leone Branch of the Universal Negro Improvement Association (UNIA) and served as President of the women's branch. The UNIA had been established in 1914 by Jamaican, Marcus Garvey. Its mission was to improve the conditions of people of African descent around the world.

Despite facing fundraising challenges in Freetown, Adelaide continued to advocate for her school for girls in Sierra Leone. In 1920, at the age of 52, Adelaide traveled to America to help raise funds for the school. In her two-year stay there, Adelaide visited 36 towns, over 50 black congregations, and formed an advisory board, which included the famous Booker T. Washington. In 1923, after her return to Sierra Leone, Adelaide finally opened the Technical and Industrial School for Girls on Gloucester Street in Freetown.

1807

After the British passed an Act to abolish the slave trade in 1807, Freetown was chosen for the Vice-Admiralty Court responsible for judicial matters involving the illegal slave-trade.

1849

Christian Missionary Society (CMS) opens a girls' secondary school, almost 4 years after the Grammar School opened in 1845 for boys. Both institutions are the first of their kind in West Africa.

Adelaide loved her African identity and expressed her African cultural pride in many ways. During a visit to Freetown by the Prince of Wales in the late 1920s, Adelaide became the exception to the rule in her fashion choice. Many of the attendees were dressed in western clothing. Adelaide, however, wore a black satin traditional lappa and an embroidered boobah, made in Pujehun. Her demonstrated pride in showcasing African culture and identity set her apart among many during her time.

She was also a very talented writer. She wrote several short stories such as 'Mista Courifer' which was featured in Langston Hughes' 'African Treasury' collection. Her legacy for girls education, advancement of women, and cultural pride continued long after her death.

THROUGHOUT SIERRA LEONE'S HISTORY OF EDUCATIONAL INSTITUTIONS, WOMEN HAVE PLAYED A ROLE IN ESTABLISHING PLATFORMS AND OPPORTUNITIES TO MAKE EDUCATION ACCESSIBLE TO GIRLS. ACCORDING TO HISTORIAN CHRISTOPHER FYFE, IN THE 1870s, A MRS. ROSE HUGHES AND MRS. ROSA FARMER OPENED 2 PRIVATE SCHOOLS FOR GIRLS IN FREETOWN. IN 1880, A WESLEYAN FEMALE INSTITUTION WAS MANAGED BY JAMES TAYLOR IN FREETOWN. TWO OF ITS PRINCIPALS WERE MRS. ELIZABETH HAMILTON, A DESCENDANT OF THE 1792 BLACK SETTLERS, AND MRS. HAZELBORG, WIFE OF CHARLES HAZELBORG, AN AFRO-WEST INDIAN BUILDER. IN MUCH EARLIER PERIODS, THOMAS AND MARIA MACFOY, A BLACK COUPLE FROM EITHER AMERICA OR THE CARIBBEAN ARRIVED IN SIERRA LEONE AS MISSIONARIES IN 1818. FOR YEARS, MARIA MACFOY MANAGED A GIRLS SCHOOLS IN WATERLOO AND

1850

William Smith Jr., Adelaide's Father was the Registrar of the Mixed Commission Court in Freetown. Thousands of enslaved Africans had been liberated and sent to Freetown since 1807.

1884

Leopold Educational Institute was established in Freetown by Rev. John Lewis-Leopold, a former tutor at the Wesleyan High School. Part of its curriculum was focused around practical and business subjects.

DR. M.C.F.
EASMON
1890-1972

Dr. McCormack Charles Farrell Easmon was born on April 11, 1890 in Accra, Gold Coast to Sierra Leonean parents Dr. John Farrell Easmon and Kathleen Annette Easmon (nee Smith). Dr. M.C.F. Easmon was a descendant of African American Settlers who arrived in Sierra Leone, in 1792.

Around 1906, Dr. Easmon attended Medical School in England. At the mere age of 22, Dr. Easmon qualified for the Membership of the Royal College of Surgeons in England and Licentiate of the Royal College of Physicians Liverpool, earning the credentials to practice medicine in the British Commonwealth. In 1913, Dr. Easmon was admitted into the Native Medical Staff and placed in Moyamba, where he learned to speak Mende fluently. He was stationed there for the next 20 years.

During World War I, Dr. Easmon served as a Lieutenant for the allied forces and was stationed in Cameroon as a medical official. Thousands of West Africans served in World War I. Many encountered an allied force with widespread discrimination. Dr. Easmon was denied certain benefits offered to other European Officers who had the same responsibilities he had. Dr. Easmon returned to Moyamba to continue his role as Native Medical Officer.

1817
John Macaulay Wilson, son of King George, Chief of Bullom was an Apothecary and at one point a Medical Official at the colonial hospital in Regent.

1871
Dr. Robert Smith was the first West African Fellow of the Royal College of Surgeons. He returned to serve as Assistant Colonial Surgeon in the Sierra Leone Colony.

In 1918, the Influenza Pandemic, noted then as the most 'catastrophic outbreak of infectious diseases in history', reached Freetown via a ship from England. Dr. Easmon's 1918 report on its impact on Moyamba and other surrounding provincial districts, especially those along the railway line, helped to understand and reduce its impact across the country. 30 million people died globally, almost 2 million in Africa and at least 2% of Sierra Leone's population. Starting in Freetown, it spread out to Dakar, Ghana, Nigeria and other places in the region. About 100,000 people perished in Ghana and 3% of the population in southern Nigeria also died.

Dr. Easmon faced racial discrimination throughout the early part of his career from the British. He was not afforded the same recognition as other European Officers for his work during World War I.

For many years, despite his exceptional credentials and experience as a Medical officer, he was refused membership into the West African Medical Staff because he was African. Ironically, in the Gold Coast, his father Dr. John Farrell Easmon had served as Chief Medical Officer in the 1890s, before the rules were suddenly changed in 1902. In fact throughout the latter part of the 19th Century, several West Africans had qualified and served in similar capacities.

Despite discrimination and repeated refusals to admit him as a member, Dr. Easmon kept trying and in the 1930s, he was finally accepted and joined the prestigious West African Medical Staff, retiring in 1945.

"DR. EASMON DEVELOPED MANY INTERESTS AND SKILLS BEYOND MEDICINE DURING HIS 20 YEARS OF WORKING IN THE SIERRA LEONE INTERIOR. HE LEARNED HOW TO SPEAK MENDE FLUENTLY AND DURING VISITS TO VARIOUS TOWNS AND CHIEFDOMS, HE COLLECTED NARRATIVES AND HISTORIES ABOUT PROMINENT FIGURES IN EACH COMMUNITY. HIS INTEREST IN SIERRA LEONE CULTURAL HERITAGE GREW AND HE LATER BECAME VERY INFLUENTIAL IN ESTABLISHING THE SIERRA LEONE NATIONAL MUSEUM."

1890s

Dr. MCF Easmon's father, John Farrell Easmon was the highest ranking African medical official at that time. He served as Chief Medical Officer in the Gold Coast in the 1880s.

1902

West African Medical Staff was created from 6 West African colonial medical departments.

His contributions to society went far beyond the medical field and into national history and heritage. His time traveling extensively and working all across Sierra Leone provided him with much interest into the heritage of the people.

In 1924, Dr. Easmon published "Sierra Leone Country Cloth" and for several years wrote publications on Paramount Chiefs in Sierra Leone. In 1947, Dr. Easmon became the first Chair of the Monuments and Cleric Commission, declaring 20 national historic sites, which are still recognized today.

He served as the first curator of the National Museum in the late 1950s and facilitated public education centered on the country's history. In the year of independence, 1961, Dr. Easmon edited the notable publication "Eminent Sierra Leoneans in the Nineteenth Century". For years, Dr. Easmon served as Chairman and member of the editorial board of Sierra Leone Society, which made countless contributions on the vast history of Sierra Leone, including the National Museum.

IN RESPONSE TO THE RACIAL POLICY OF THE WEST AFRICAN MEDICAL STAFF (WAMS), SIERRA LEONEAN DR. MICHAEL LEWIS JARRETT, WROTE A REPORT IN 1913 FOLLOWING A REQUEST BY THE ANTI-SLAVERY AND ABORIGINES PROTECTION (ASAP) SOCIETY. THE REQUEST WAS TO LIST QUALIFIED NATIVE AFRICAN MEDICAL MEN WHO HAD STUDIED IN THE UNITED KINGDOM AND IRELAND, AND GAINED ADMISSION INTO GOVERNMENT SERVICE SINCE THE 1860S. ACCORDING TO JARRETT'S REPORT, THERE HAD BEEN 9 FROM SIERRA LEONE, 1 FROM THE GAMBIA, 5 FROM THE GOLD COAST, AND 8 FROM LAGOS. THE LIST FROM SIERRA LEONE INCLUDED DR. HERBERT BANKOLE-BRIGHT AND DR. ISHMAEL CHARLES PRATT. EVEN THOUGH SEVERAL OF THESE AFRICAN PHYSICIANS HAD BEEN MEMBERS OF THE COLONIAL MEDICAL SERVICE BY THE TURN OF THE 20TH CENTURY, NONE OF THEM WOULD BE ALLOWED MEMBERSHIP IN THE NEWLY FORMED WAMS OF 1902 DUE TO THE DISCRIMATION IN ITS MEMBERSHIP POLICY.

1914
World War I begins, lasting until 1918. According to UNESCO, about 2.5 million Africans served in some capacity during the war. Sierra Leoneans from the interior also took part in this war.

1961
Sierra Leone gained independence. National culture and heritage were some of the unifying factors promoting nationalism.

ADAMA
SALLIE KARGBO

1983 - 2018

Adama Kargbo will be remembered as an elegant and gifted fashion designer who made her mark in the world of high fashion before her untimely death at age 34. She was born Sallie Adama Kargbo in New Jersey on March 5, 1983 to Hon. Momodu Kargbo and Jennifer Kargbo from Sierra Leone. She grew up between Sierra Leone, Ethiopia and the United States. A friend described her as a talented and forward-thinking Sierra Leonean fashion designer determined to conquer the world of fashion on her own terms.

Adama trained in Paris and New York. She graduated in 2006 with a Bachelor of Arts in Fashion/Apparel Design from Parsons School of Design in Paris, one of the world's leading art and design schools. After graduation, Adama returned to New York to begin her career, working at fashion magazines and style campaigns for different brands. In 2008, she decided it was time to pursue her dream of building her own brand, with inspiration from her home in Africa. Adama initially focused on the African market in the diaspora who wore traditional African materials in everyday settings and in modern, fashion forward styles.

She moved back to Sierra Leone and co-founded the fashion brand, ASCHOBI. This daring step was the first of many that would launch her into the limelight as the fashion designer, Adama Kai.

1812

Liberated Africans were sent to form villages of their own on a hill above the deserted Granville Town. They named it Kissy Town, suggesting they came from Kisi country, north of the Melakori river.

1889

Samuel Coleridge Taylor (Black Mahler) of Sierra Leonean and British parentage, was a talented musician who composed classical piano inspired by African themes. He is still celebrated around the world.

At an early stage in her career, Adama Kai expressed her vision for a fashion brand rooted in the history and diverse culture of Africa. That brand became ASCHOBI and was born from extensive training and expertise within the luxury fashion industry. Adama Kai once said, "the combination of my past experiences has allowed me to push my imagination on being innovative and practical in the decisions I have had to make. I am adaptable to newer aspects of the design industry."

"IN THE SAME WAY THAT RALPH LAUREN STANDS FOR AMERICA, CHANEL FOR FRANCE, AND VERSACE FOR ITALY, I WANT ASCHOBI TO STAND FOR AFRICAN FASHION."
~ ADAMA KAI

Adama Kai opened her startup company ASCHOBI out of a small storefront on Pademba Road in downtown Freetown. The brand grew through local and international events while nurturing her connections in the fashion industry in New York and Paris. As her company expanded, the goals evolved.

She collaborated with gara producers in the city of Makeni to strengthen their production skills and drive innovation in the traditional fashion industry. In working with these artisans she raised the connections between the work they do, textile design, and the very foundation of fashion. This collaboration inspired the Aschobi signature print. Adama Kai became a champion of celebrating Sierra Leonean fashion and textiles on the world stage. These entrepreneurial activities enabled her to pursue her dream of providing the high fashion (haute couture) industry a hint of Africa's inspiration by way of the print she created.

In 2012, she made an impressionable entrance into the high fashion industry. A review of her initial collection described it as "a celebration of the career minded African woman who balances family, community, and work obligations with grace, elegance, and beauty. In a poetic way, the ASCHOBI woman that Adama had fashioned in those years with her design while in Sierra Leone were Maya Angelou's phenomenal woman."

1893
Freetown City Council was established by an Ordinance in this year. The first mayoral election was held two years later in August. Sir Samuel Lewis won and became the first Mayor of Freetown.

1946
West African Airways Corporation (WAAC) was established and jointly owned by the colonial governments of Sierra Leone, The Gambia, Ghana and Nigeria.

More than a decade of dressing men and women with the finest custom styles both in Sierra Leone and around the globe led Adama to the pinnacle of world fashion, Paris Fashion Week. On October 6th of 2012, she presented her Spring - Summer 2013 ASCHOBI collection at Le Bristol hotel; clothing styles inspired by the myth of the underwater spirit, Mami Wata. That day, she expressed what she had achieved at age 30 with her signature smile and radiant glow.

At 34 and just as she began to lay the foundation for her next stage of fashion innovation, Adama Kai passed away from a medical complication in late January, 2018 in New York. She continues to live through the brand ASCHOBI. That hint of African-insipired print and fashion forward design will keep her alive at home and around the world.

ADAMA KAI SPOKE OF HER INSPIRATION - MAMI WATA - AT HER 2013 SPRING-SUMMER ASCHOBI SHOW. IN HER WORDS,

" THE INSPIRATION FOR THIS COLLECTION WAS FOR ME TO BRING THIS SEA CREATURE FROM UP UNDER THE EARTH UNTO THE JUNGLE OF SKYSCRAPERS THAT I AM IN NOW, COMING FROM MY HOME COUNTY TO EUROPE. SO IT WAS ABOUT ADAPTING HER TO HER NEW ENVIRONMENT, PREPARING HER FOR THE NEW TASK THAT LAY AHEAD. AT THE SAME TIME STRIPPING HER OF ALL THINGS FROM HER PAST TO CLEAN SIMPLE LINES, CLEAN CURVE LINES AND ALLOWING WHAT DROVE HER TO THE FOREFRONT IN THE PAST TO BE WHAT IS HER FOUNDATION FOR THE FUTURE...

...FOR ME IT WAS THE BEST EXPERIENCE TO DO MY OWN PRINT AND LIKE NO ONE ELSE IS GOING TO HAVE IT AND WHEN PEOPLE SEE IT THEY WILL KNOW IT IS THE ASCHOBI PRINT. FOR ME I HAVE ALWAYS WANTED THAT, TO SET MYSELF APART. THIS IS ONE OF THE WAYS PEOPLE DO IT TODAY. SO, TO BE ABLE TO DO THAT LIKE ALL MY OTHER PEERS IN THE INDUSTRY IT LETS ME KNOW I AM NO LONGER WHERE I WAS BEFORE. "

1970

Tiwai Island was recognised as a special biosphere for wildlife conservation. Tiwai in Mende means big island and Tiwai Island is Sierra Leone's first community conservation programme with one of the highest concentration and diversity of primates.

1960

Dr Davidson Nicol was the first to analyse the breakdown of insulin in the human body, a discovery which was a breakthrough for the treatment of diabetes.

DR. SHEIK
UMAR KHAN

1975 - 2014

D r. Sheik Umar Khan was born in 1975 in the Northern Province of Sierra Leone. He received medical training and graduated in 2001 from the College of Medicine and Allied Health Sciences, a branch of the University of Sierra Leone. He began his career as a Tropical Medicine and Infectious Disease Physician.

In 2004, Dr. Khan took over the position of Chief Physician at the Kenema Government Hospital's Lassa Fever Research program. The position was previously held by Dr. Aniru Conteh who had done pioneering work at the Lassa Fever laboratory. The laboratory was based at the Nixon Memorial Hospital in Segbwema, in the eastern part of Sierra Leone.

Kenema, in the eastern province of Sierra Leone, served as one of the most important centers for lassa fever research in the world. In the mid-1970s, a research scientist from the American Center for Disease Control had opened the research laboratory in Segbwema. Operations were transferred to Guinea during the civil-war in 1991, while Dr. Conteh and others moved the research laboratory to Kenema Government Hospital. This research facility became the only lassa fever isolation unit in the world.

1792
A fever broke out on ships carrying black settlers sailing from Nova Scotia to settle in Freetown. Of the nearly 1200 settlers, about 800 fell ill and many died.

1836
Yellow Fever epidemic entered Freetown on a timber merchant ship. Many residents died as a result. Leeches from Bullom was one of the remedies used to treat the disease.

Sierra Leone has experienced a share of epidemics and contagious diseases. In 1792, small-pox killed a large number of the black American settlers who had recently arrived in Freetown. Yellow-fever breakouts had been a constant issue. In 1829, an infected ship from Fernando Po entered Sierra Leone, bringing the disease, which spread through the European community. Other instances of yellow-fever occurred in 1836, 1839, and 1859.

In 1918, during the Spanish Flu pandemic, about 20,000 of Freetown's population, or 60% were affected. Back in Moyamba, Easmon reported 767 deaths in Ponietta District and 2 nearby Chiefdoms. There were high death rates reported for the Northern and Southern regions of Sierra Leone. Sierra Leone would experience more than a fair share of epidemics for almost another half a century, including a cholera outbreak in 1970 and one of its worst cholera outbreak in 2012, with over 19,000 cases.

"DURING THE EBOLA EPIDEMIC, OVER 28,000 CASES WERE REPORTED ACROSS SIERRA LEONE, LIBERIA, AND GUINEA. OVER 11,000 PATIENTS DIED BECAUSE OF THE DISEASE, WHILE OVER 2,000 RECOVERED."

In 2014, between May and July, the Ebola epidemic had its first reported cases in Sierra Leone in the towns of Kailahun and Segbwema, both in the eastern province. Dr. Khan and a Professor from the Microbiology and Immunology Department at Tulane University School of Medicine diagnosed some of the first cases in Sierra Leone. News of the epidemic went global and several international medical personnel traveled to the region to help. The world looked unto the Mano river union countries of Guinea, Sierra Leone, and Liberia as healthcare workers were seen in personal protective equipment, attending to sick patients.

Dr. Khan treated hundreds of Ebola patients in the early stages of the outbreak. He refused to turn away patients even though his facility was not fully equipped to handle such a large number of infected patients. His courage and empathy was revered throughout the country and internationally.

1858

Dr. W. Broughton Davies and Dr. James Africanus Beale Horton were some of the first Sierra Leonean Medical Doctors. Horton was from Gloucester and Davies from Wellington.

1874

According to Historian Iyamide Thomas, Sierra Leonean, Dr. James A.B. Horton in his publication "The Diseases of Tropical Climates and Their Treatment", detailed the first written account of what would later be called 'Sickle Cell'.

Healthcare institutions in Sierra Leone suffered a devastating blow during the epidemic. Over 8,000 people were infected and over 1,800 died. Many of the country's valued healthcare workers became victims. A State of Emergency was issued which resulted in several public-private sector and community groups participating in efforts to control the outbreak.

On July 22nd, 2014, Dr. Khan tested positive for ebola. At the time, a treatment for Ebola called ZMapp was the only potential treatment readily available. A debate followed, whether to give the experimental drug to Dr. Khan and a controversial decision was made against using the drug to treat him. Dr. Khan passed seven days later from the disease at the Ebola Treatment Centre in Kailahun.

IN 2014, TIME MAGAZINE NAMED EBOLA FIGHTERS AS ITS "PERSON OF THE YEAR" FOR THEIR COURAGE AND EFFORTS IN CONTROLLING THE EPIDEMIC. AMONG THOSE LISTED WERE NURSES, PHYSICIANS, SCIENTISTS, AND CAREGIVERS. TIME MAGAZINE WAS ONE OF THE MAJOR INTERNATIONAL NEWS OUTLETS TO ANNOUNCE THAT DR. KHAN HAD CONTRACTED THE DEADLY DISEASE.

1926

Milton Margai becomes the first Sierra Leonean from the Protectorate to earn a medical degree from the University of Durham. He worked as a physician for the colonial administration between 1927-1949.

2012

A cholera outbreak in Sierra Leone left about 22,000 people ill and over 200 deaths.

JOHN
KIZELL

1760s - 1800s

John Kizell is believed to have been born in the Gallinas region, southeastern Sierra Leone, around 1760. As a young boy in the early 1770s, he was captured, enslaved and transported to Charleston, South Carolina where he was forced to work as a slave on a plantation. During those oppressive years, he managed to learn how to read and write, becoming competent in both. During the American Revolutionary War, he joined the British side of the American Revolutionary War.

In 1783, John traveled with about 3,000 other black loyalists from America to Nova Scotia, Canada to settle there. In Birchtown, Nova Scotia, John Kizell and his family received several acres of land as part of their reward for his service during the war. He became a farmer in Nova Scotia, where all three of his children were born.

By 1791, a new proposal had been promoted to the settlers in Nova Scotia, to relocate and start a new settlement in Africa. In 1792, John Kizell landed in Sierra Leone with nearly 1,200 black settlers from America. Together, they cleared a settlement near the Sierra Leone river and named it Freetown. John Kizell had returned back to the region of his former home that he had been enslaved almost 20 years earlier.

1775

The American Revolutionary War begins between American Patriots and the British. The outcome was the United States of America.

1783

Over 3,000 black loyalists left America to settle in Nova Scotia, Canada. Many of them had fled enslavement and joined the British, receiving their freedom in return.

By 1796, John Kizell along with some of the Settlers, had built their own boat and started trading as merchants from Freetown into the hinterland. John Kizell lived in the settlement for years, owning several properties and land in Freetown.

On a trip to Sierra Leone in 1811, Paul Cuffee, an African American Ship Navigator, met with Kizell and other leaders in Freetown. Together, along with some of the Settlers, they formed the Friendly Society of Sierra Leone. John Kizell served as President and worked to establish trading relationships between Sierra Leone and African Americans. Cuffee traveled again to Sierra Leone around 1815 with about 38 African American emigrants. Kizell's work with Paul Cuffee led to plans by the American Colonization Society (ACS), responsible for the emigration of African Americans to Africa.

"IN 1811, PAUL CUFFEE, AN AFRICAN AMERICAN SHIP NAVIGATOR TRAVELLED TO SIERRA LEONE, SEEKING TO ESTABLISH BUSINESS RELATIONS BETWEEN AFRICAN AMERICANS AND SETTLERS IN FREETOWN. CUFFEE'S FATHER WAS A FREED SLAVE BEIEVED TO BE OF ASHANTI ORIGIN. HIS MOTHER WAS A WAMPANOEG NATIVE AMERICAN. BORN IN MASSACHUSETTS, CUFFEE BOUGHT AND BUILT HIS OWN SHIPS, SAILING ALONG THE AMERICAN COAST, CARIBBEAN ISLANDS, EUROPE AND AFRICA. HE WAS ONE OF THE FIRST TO DEVELOP AN ALL BLACK NAVIGATION CREW AND FLEET OF SHIPS."

In 1820, John Kizell served as a mediator between the first African American settlers sent by the ACS and chiefs for negotiations to form a settlement in the region. Over 80 black settlers from America arrived and settled temporarily near Kizell's hometown. Among them was Rev. Daniel Coker, an African American from Maryland who was one of the founding members of the American Methodist Episcopalian (AME) Church in America.

About a year or two later, more black American settlers arrived from Virginia. A few of this new group of settlers remained in Sierra Leone, while a large number moved to Cape Mesurado and established the new settlement of Liberia.

1791
1,200+ of the black settlers in Nova Scotia, left and founded the settlement of Freetown.

1811
Paul Cuffee travels to Freetown. His crew were mostly black, and he owned his own fleet of ships, rare for a black man at that time.

John Kizell's life was a journey of adventures. He endured slavery, a revolutionary war, lived a free man on two continents, and returned safely back to his hometown, a literate and enterprising settler. His efforts helped establish two settlements that are still thriving today.

THE AMERICAN COLONIZATION SOCIETY (ACS) WAS FOUNDED IN 1816. ITS MAIN GOAL WAS TO HELP AFRICAN AMERICAN EMIGRANTS RESETTLE IN AFRICA. PAUL CUFFEE WAS A KEY INFLUENCER TO THE EARLY STAGES OF THE ACS. IN 1820, REV. DANIEL COKER, ONE OF THE FOUNDING MEMBERS OF THE AMERICAN METHODIST EPISCOPAL CHURCH (AME) WAS PART OF THE FIRST MAJOR GROUP SENT TO SETTLE IN AFRICA. REV. COKER WAS BORN IN 1780 IN MARYLAND TO AN AFRICAN AMERICAN ENSLAVED FATHER AND HIS MOTHER WAS AN ENGLISH INDENTURED SERVANT. IN BALTIMORE, BEFORE 1800, REV. COKER HAD FOUNDED ONE OF THE FIRST BLACK METHODIST CHURCHES IN BALTIMORE AND IN 1807 HE FOUNDED THE BETHEL CITY CHARITY SCHOOL FOR NEGROES.

THE GROUP OF EMIGRANTS THAT ARRIVED IN SIERRA LEONE IN 1820 INTENDED TO ESTABLISH A SETTLEMENT OF THEIR OWN AROUND THE SHERBRO REGION. AFTER MEETING STRONG HOSTILITY FROM LOCAL CHIEFS, REV. COKER CHOSE TO RESETTLE IN FREETOWN AND BECAME EMPLOYED BY THE COLONIAL ADMINISTRATION AS A MANAGER OF SOME OF THE LIBERATED AFRICAN VILLAGES. BY 1827, HE WAS IN CHARGE OF WATERLOO VILLAGE AND AROUND 1833, HASTINGS. HIS SON, DANIEL COKER JR., LATER MANAGED A HOTEL IN THE HEART OF FREETOWN.

1820
American Colonization Society (ACS) sends its first group of African American Emigrants.

1824
The Colony at Cape Mesurado is renamed Monrovia.

MADAM WOKI
MASSAQUOI
1870s - 1971

Paramount Chief Woki Massaqoui of the Vai people of Gallinas (Vai) country was born around 1871 and died as a centenarian in 1971. Madam Woki Massaquoi of Gallines Perri chiefdom was its longest serving female Paramount Chief. She carried the authority that came with the seven-arched crown of Massaquoi, the ruling family, from 1925 to 1971. The chiefdom was created by joining the neighbouring chiefdoms of Gallinas and Perri in 1945. The center of the chiefdom is the town of Blama Massaquoi in Pujehun District.

The Gallinas people trace their origins to a hunter named Gideon, who migrated from the Mali Empire (1235-1670). He was a great hunter, and first settled at Gangba village in Mano Sakrim chiefdom. He married and had a son named Kadehen, who left the chiefdom and settled at Dumagbay village in Pujehun District.

Kadehen had a son named Siaka, who then settled in Gendema, Soro Gbema chiefdom and later asserted control over the chiefdom in a series of wars during the mid 19th century. Gendema became the capital city of the Gallinas.

1813

A shipload of Vai people were sent to Hogbrook (Regent) where the governor of the day had planned a village. Adjoining towns were also settled by Jolof, Mandinka and Susu recaptives, each forming their own towns.

1920

Gola Forest Reserves was established and expanded several times. Today it encompasses seven chiefdoms and is home to over 300 species of birds.

At the time of King Siaka, two hunters named Kamageh and Torgbah arrived in the chiefdom and presented him with the gift of ivory in exchange for a piece of land. Kamageh gave birth to Vandi Guya who became the first ruler of a semi-autonomous region in Peri. This became Perri chiefdom.

In 1882, the king and chiefs of Gallinas ceded a piece of coastal territory to the British government when they controlled Sierra Leone. Gallinas was recognized as a territory of an independent Kingdom of and for the Vai people. It occupied lands that covered southeastern Sierra Leone and western Liberia. The term Gallinas, which applies only to that portion of the Vai country that is situated in Sierra Leone today, was derived from the Portuguese word galinha (hen). The name was probably given to the territory because of the great number of guinea fowls found there by Portuguese sailors.

"WE ARE MOTHERS OF THE MEN, A NEW CONSTITUTION SHOULD CLEARLY DEFINE THE STATUS OF WOMEN." ~ DAILYMAIL MARCH 16, 1960.

The original inhabitants of the territory called it Massaquoi, and this name was chosen because a member of the Massaquoi family played the most important role in its founding. The term massaquoi, meaning king, was adopted by Siaka. King George III of England Bestowed the Crown on King Siaka Massaquoi for the Gallinas People in 1814. The seven-arched crown with a medal titled George III was later passed to his son, Prince Manna.

The Prince succeeded his father in 1843 became very wealthy through the sale of fellow Africans to a notorious Portuguese slaver. King Manna's successor was his brother Jaya and Jaya was succeeded by their sister Madam Yata in 1890. Thereafter there was much dissension in the region between the various sub-chiefs, as each wanted to become Massaquoi. This dissension allowed slavery to continue long after it was abolished in 1807. The British signed a final treaty with the Gallinas in 1885 to end slave trading in its territory.

1938
The West African Youth League was the first political movement to elect five women into its central committee on a platform of equality.

1940
Saw the creation of two women trade unions; Sierra Leone Market Women's Union led by Mary M. Martyn and Washer Women's Union by Christiana England.

The Vai are a Mande ethnic group known for their indigenous syllabic writing system known as Vai syllabary which was developed in the 1820s by Momolu Duwalu Bukele of Jondu and other tribal elders. The Vai script was found to be an emergent writing system that inspired the creation of multiple new indigenous writing systems across the West African region.

In 1925 Madam Woki Massaquoi became Paramount Chief of Gallines Chiefdom. The story around the amalgamation of Gallines and neighbouring Perri Chiefdom in 1945 has yet to be explained beyond the administrative action by the colonial government. Madam Woki Massaquoi's chieftaincy covered the amalgamated chiefdoms and was named Gallines Perri Chiefdom. Queen Elizabeth II designated her a Member of the British Empire (MBE) in 1968. Paramount Chief Woki Massaquoi carried the authority that came with the seven-arched crown of Massaquoi ruling family until her death in 1971.

LITERATURE ABOUT COASTAL COMMUNITIES STARTING AROUND THE MID-1400s AS WELL AS ETHNOGRAPHIC AND LINGUISTIC STUDIES IN THE RECENT DECADE, AFFIRMS THE RICH DIVERSITY OF AFRICAN LANGUAGES OF SIERRA LEONE. THIS ILLUSTRATES THE RICH DIVERSITY OF THE CULTURE. THE TWENTY LANGUAGES SPOKEN WITHIN SIERRA LEONE ARE: BOM, BULLOM, ENGLISH, FULA, GOLA, LIMBA, LOKO, KISSI, KONO, KORANKO (KURANKO), KRIM, KRIO, KRU (KLAO), MANDINGO (MALINKE, MANINKA), MENDE, SHERBRO, SOSO (SUSU), TEMNE, VAI (GALLINAS), YALUNKA

1951

Sierra Leone Women's Movement was formed for the status of Sierra Leone women in the colony and protectorate by Constance Cummings-John.

1958

Ella Koblo Gulama became the Paramount Chief of Marampa Masimera Chiefdom and was elected to one of the twelve seats reserved for Paramount chiefs in Parliament.

AHMED
JANKA NABAY

1964 - 2018

Ahmed Janka Nabay introduced the unique festive Bubu music sounds to our nation and the world. His two music albums with an international label remains a testament to his legacy. He was born to Mandingo and Temne parents on Jan. 5, 1964 in Sedu, a rural village within the Port Loko District. His family relocated to Makeni first and later settled in Freetown when he was 14 years. Ahmed began his music career playing reggae music and later went on to play Bubu music.

Bubu is a traditional Temne music sound that is played by a group of musicians using hollow bamboo flutes, metal pipes, and drums as they lead a parade slowly through a village or community. Janka Nabay explained to his audiences that Bubu is a centuries-old folk music with origins that precede Islam arriving in Sierra Leone.

The Bubu King, as he was called, sang in Temne, Krio, English, and Arabic. During his early years, he nurtured his talent by performing at many music festivals, ceremonial celebrations, such as Sierra Leone's Independence Day carnivals and holy month of Ramadan processions.

1897

Victoria Park opened on the site used for many celebrations along with its adjacent field, the "old burying ground" and dailymail fairgrounds. The Park is the only 'green space' in the center of Freetown.

1905

On May 24th an ordinance to provide for the punishment for practising Fangay in the Colony and Protectorate of Sierra Leone was promulgated. Fangay was a practice claiming to have supernatural powers.

In the early 1990s, he wrote "Dance to the Bubu" for a nationwide song contest, with lyrics that proclaimed, "It's an ancient style of music, but when you try it you will never leave it." Against the backdrop of a civil war, his songs for peace became hits as the war tore the nation apart. Janka Nabay's musical efforts to champion the cause of peace is captured in "Sabanoh" his well known and popular Bubu music song. Years later, he recounted that he left Sierra Leone during the war years in the middle of advocating for peace. Regrettably, the rebels camouflaged themselves as a Bubu group playing 'Sabanoh' while entering the villages and drawing innocent villagers to congregate and dance before turning on them. His songs promoted culture in good times, and peace during the civil war years.

"BUBU IS AN OLD, OLD MUSIC, BUT PEOPLE DON'T KNOW ABOUT IT. YOU CAN ADD NEW THINGS INTO THE BEAT IF YOU KNOW IT REALLY WELL, AND MAKE YOUR OWN SOUND OUT OF IT."

Janka Nabay emigrated in 2002 to New York City on an artist visa. The first few years were hard, as an immigrant artist, however he found a way to make his talent known. Eventually he started a band, the Bubu Gang, and they began recording sessions. In the Bubu Gang he collaborated with four other musicians and they embarked on a journey of introducing Bubu music to an international audience. The band became popular and played in festivals throughout the United States of America. In 2012 Janka Nabay announced that they had signed a three-album record deal with record label, Luaka Bop. The Bubu Gang went on to record two albums; En Yay Sah (I'm Scared) in 2012 and Build Music in 2017. A music review explained that his work as "Nabay took the speedy beat of music that had been heard for centuries in parades and celebrations and transferred it to western instruments. Janka-Nabay had something to share with the world from then on."

In 2017 he went on to do his first music tour in Europe. At the end of this tour, he made a decision to complete his third album in Sierra Leone. Ahmed Janka Nabay returned home with a vision to enrich his music and produce his third album locally for his international label.

1912
Ebenezer Calender, a Krio palm-wine musician, was born. He popularized Krio gumbe and palm-wine music in Sierra Leone and West Africa.

1947
Tingi Hills Forest Reserve was established. Over 200 species of birds have been recorded in the area and the reserve is also home to western baboons and forest elephants.

Sadly, he died on April 2, 2018 in Freetown before he could complete it. Ahmed Janka Nabay died young but left a music legacy for other young Sierra Leoneans to build upon. He showed how to collaborate with other musicians around the world to make something new that is inspired by Sierra Leonean music and culture.

EID AL-FITR IS A NATIONAL HOLIDAY IN SIERRA LEONE THAT OCCURS ON THE FIRST DAY OF THE ISLAMIC MONTH OF SHAWWAL, IMMEDIATELY FOLLOWING THE HOLY MONTH OF RAMADAN AND MONTH-LONG PERIOD OF FASTING, PRAYER AND DEVOTION. DEVOUT MUSLIMS FAST FROM SUNRISE TO SUNSET FOR 29 OR 30 DAYS STRAIGHT. THEY WILL STAY UP LATE TO EAT A LITTLE, PRAY, AND RECITE KORANIC VERSES EACH NIGHT. THIS PERIOD IS CALLED "TAHAJUD". EID AL-FITR ENCOMPASSES THE DESIRE AND CHALLENGE TO KEEP UP THE DISCIPLINE AND DEVOTION LEARNED DURING RAMADAN ALL YEAR LONG. ON THIS DAY, MUSLIMS ARE RELEASED FROM RAMADAN'S STRICTURES AND GIVEN THE CHANCE TO AGAIN ENJOY THE FULL BOUNTY OF LIFE. LANTERN PARADE BEGAN IN THE 1840S WHEN MUSLIMS IN THE LIBERATED AFRICAN COMMUNITY OF FOURAH BAY AND FULA TOWN MADE A PROCESSION FROM THE EAST TO THE GOVERNMENT HOUSE AS THE CONCLUDING CELEBRATION OF RAMADAN.

1967

Tangains Festival was borne out of cultural and music revival in the mid 60s. It is now a month long, day and night festival of food, culture, music and trade each December.

2009

Ma Dengn Beach Festival was conceived out of a collective need to celebrate and promote Sierra Leonean culture. Ma Dengn comes from the Kuranko dialect and mean "Let's meet" or "Let's come together."

DR. DAVIDSON
NICOL

1924 - 1994

Davidson Sylvester Hector Willoughby Nicol was born on 14 September 1924 in Bathurst, Western Area, Sierra Leone. He attended primary school in Nigeria. On August 11, 1950, he married Marjorie Esmé and they had five children. Dr Davidson Nicol retired in 1991 at the age of 67 and relocated to Cambridge U.K., where he died three years later at the age of 70. Early in his career, he taught at the Prince of Wales School in Freetown, and later earned a scholarship to study at Christ's College, Cambridge University U.K. where he graduated with a first class BA in Natural Science in 1947. He proceeded to study for a medical degree at Barts and The London School of Medicine and Dentistry.

In the early 1950s, he taught at Ibadan University Medical School, researching topical malnutrition, before returning to Cambridge in 1954. Three years later, he was named the first African Fellow of Christ's College and went to the college to do research on insulin. He published two research papers, "The Mechanism of Action of Insulin" and "The Structure of Human Insulin". in 1960. His research to analyse the breakdown of insulin in the human body was a breakthrough discovery for the treatment of diabetes. He returned to Freetown in 1958 to take up the Pathologist position in the Government of Sierra Leone.

1825

Former villages of Leopold and Bathurst in the mountain were amalgamated and named Bathurst.

1827

The Church Missionary Society (CMS) founded Fourah Bay College, the first westernized college in West Africa. The first black Principal of the college was Rev. Edward Jones, an African American minister.

In 1960, Dr. Davidson Nicol became the first native Principal of Fourah Bay College in Freetown for the next eight years. Under his leadership, the university expanded its infrastructure and academic programs. Dr. Nicol went on to be the Chairman (1964–68), and as Vice-Chancellor (1966-68) at the University of Sierra Leone. He was made a distinguished Honorary Fellow at his alma mater Christ's College, England. He was also a visiting Professor of International Studies at the University of California (1987–88) and University of South Carolina (1990–91).

"IN 1964 HE WAS AWARDED THE C.M.G; COMPANION OF THE MOST DISTINGUISHED ORDER OF SAINT MICHAEL AND SAINT GEORGE. AN HONOUR CONFERRED MOSTLY ON OFFICIALS IN COLONIAL AFFAIRS, FOREIGN-SERVICE OFFICERS AND DIPLOMATS, AND OTHERS WHO HAVE PERFORMED IMPORTANT DUTIES IN COMMONWEALTH COUNTRIES."

Dr. Davidson Nicol also wrote many short stories. He published in 1965 two short stories titled "Two African Tales" and "The Truly Married Woman", under the name Abioseh Nicol and a biography of Africanus Horton. He published poetry, music, and scholarly works. Dr. Davidson Nicol advocated for the creation of an organization of Africa Unity in his 1963 insightful book "Africa a Subjective View". The book was based on his week long lecture at the University of Ghana that provided a perspective on African Politicians as well as critics and lovers of Africa. In this book, he expressed a new and pivotal concept of the role and formation of an Organization of African Unity. He emphasized that the organization should focus on health and education to the benefit of all member states. His last piece of published work was "Creative Women" in 1982.

Dr. Davidson Nicol left academia in 1968 to become the Permanent Representative of Sierra Leone to the United Nations, which he served for three years. In 1971, Dr. Nicol became the High Commissioner to the United Kingdom, and in the following year became the Under-Secretary-General of the United Nations and served until 1982.

1868
A.B C Sibthorpe, an alumni of Fourah Bay College, produced "The History of Sierra Leone" hoping to provide a portrait to rising generations.

1921
Ernest D. Morgan passed the qualifying exam to become Sierra Leone's first certified Druggist with Certificate No.1 issued by Governor Wilkinson. He began his practice in Blama, serving the Provinces and went on to build the successful Morgan Pharmacy chain in Sierra Leone.

During his time at the United Nations, he served as Under-Secretary General and as head of the United Nations Institute for Training and Research (UNITAR). Dr. Nicol was appointed as Ambassador of Sierra Leone to Norway, Sweden, and Denmark. He served as President of the United Nations Security Council in September 1970, and World Federation of United Nations Associations from 1983 to 1987.

THE DECLARATION OF THE PROTECTORATE IN 1896 BEGAN INDIRECT RULE, WHEREBY TRADITIONAL RULERS WOULD GOVERN AS 'NATIVE LEADERS' UNDER THE AUSPICES OF THE GOVERNOR HEADING THE COLONIAL ADMINISTRATION. THE SYSTEM OF LOCAL GOVERNMENT IN POST-INDEPENDENCE SIERRA LEONE TRACES ITS HISTORICAL ORIGIN, AT LEAST IN PART, TO THE SYSTEM OF INDIRECT RULE THAT EXISTED IN THE PROTECTORATE DURING THE COLONIAL ERA. INITIALLY, THE PROTECTORATE OF SIERRA LEONE COMPRISED FIVE ADMINISTRATIVE DISTRICTS: KARENE, RONIETTA, BANDAJUMA, PANGUMA, AND KOINADUGU, EACH OF WHICH WERE GOVERNED BY A DISTRICT COMMISSIONER, APPOINTED BY THE COLONIAL GOVERNOR. BETWEEN 1898-1921, IT WAS THROUGH ONLY FIVE SUCH DISTRICT COMMISSIONERS THAT THE COLONIAL GOVERNMENT MAINTAINED ITS 'RULE' OVER THE PROTECTORATE. SIERRA LEONE'S COLONIAL GOVERNMENT DIVIDED THE TRADITIONAL RULERS INTO THREE CATEGORIES. THESE WERE: (1) PARAMOUNT CHIEFS; (2) SUB-CHIEFS OR SECTION CHIEFS, WHO WERE SUBSERVIENT TO A PARAMOUNT CHIEF AND RULED ONLY A SECTION OF THAT PARAMOUNT CHIEF'S TERRITORY; AND (3) HEADMEN, WHO WERE THE HEADS OF VILLAGE COMMUNITIES. THE COLONIAL GOVERNMENT ALSO DESIGNATED THE TERRITORIES OF EACH PARAMOUNT CHIEF AS CHIEFDOMS. THE DISTRICT COMMISSIONERS WOULD SUPERVISE THE PARAMOUNT CHIEFS OF THESE CHIEFDOMS, AND UNDER SUCH SUPERVISION, THE PARAMOUNT CHIEFS WOULD RULE THE LOCALS WITH THE AID OF THEIR ATTENDANTS, CALLED SPEAKERS, OR THROUGH SUB-CHIEFS; IN THIS WAY, A SYSTEM OF INDIRECT RULE WAS FORMED.

1960

Dr Davidson Nicol was the first to analyse the breakdown of insulin in the human body, a discovery which was a breakthrough for the treatment of diabetes.

1963

The Organization of African Union (OAU) was founded by 32 African Head of states with the main aim of bringing the African nations together. It is headquartered in Addis Ababa, Ethiopia. Davidson Nicol articulated the agenda for OAU to be health and education in his 1963 lecture Series in Ghana.

SENGBEH

PIEH

1800s - 1879

Sengbeh Pieh was captured illegally by African slave traders in 1839. He was taken to a nearby village in Gallinas (Vai) country where he spent three days with a man called Mayagilalo, the boss of his captors. Mayagilalo was indebted to the son of the Vai King, Manna Siaka, and so he gave over Sengbeh to him as a settlement. After staying in Siaka's town for a month, Sengbeh was marched to Lomboko, a notorious slave-trading island near Sulima on the Sierra Leone Atlantic coast. Sengbeh was imprisoned on the Portuguese slave ship Tecora with 110 others and they were shipped in March 1839 to Havana, Cuba.

Four months later, on June 30, 1839, he was on a subsequent voyage on a ship named La Amistad with other enslaved Africans leaving Havana to Puerto Principe. Sengbeh used a loose spike he had removed from the deck to unshackle himself and his fellow Africans. Sengbeh and others armed themselves with cane knives and took over the ship. He ordered the ship's captain to sail eastward towards Africa but during the night winds drove the ship towards the United States.

1817

Le Louis case at the Freetown Court of Vice Admiralty ended enforcement of British ban on the slave trade at seas and resulted in the creation of the Mixed Commission agreement of all states to withdraw from the trade.

1819

Courts of Mixed Commission was the first international court in Freetown to prosecute slavers and settle liberated Africans involving Sierra Leonean officials from the Colony.

The Amistad was taken into custody by the United States (U.S) authority and Sengbeh Pieh and his fellow Africans were eventually tried for mutiny and killing officers on the ship, in a famous case known as United States v. The Amistad. In 1839, the U.S. anti-slavery movement was in disarray, with divergent views on several issues. The Amistad case provided a focal point for rallying the many groups of abolitionists, as they all came out in defense of the Africans. Their ordeal was recounted in many newspapers at the time. Sengbeh Pieh was called Joseph Cinqué in the US and became the famous West African man of the Mende people who led a revolt on the Spanish slave ship La Amistad. The case reached the U.S. Supreme Court, where Cinqué and his fellow Africans were found to have rightfully defended themselves from being enslaved through the illegal Atlantic slave trade and were released in 1841.

"WE ARE NOT BORN IN AFRICA, AFRICA IS BORN IN US."
THE INALIENABLE CONNECTION OF PEOPLE IN AFRICA AND PEOPLE OF AFRICAN DESCENT AROUND THE WORLD EXPRESSED BY MAROON CHIEF, MICHAEL GRIZZLE TRELAWNY JAMAICA TOWN AT THE 2016 TREATY DAY CELEBRATION.

Farmington, an early abolitionist town in Connecticut invited Sengbeh and others to reside. The abolitionists helped raise money for their return to Sierra Leone by having Joseph Cinqué go on a speaking tour. In 1842, they returned to Freetown with missionary friends who came to set up a mission in his hometown. Unfortunately, the Mende civil war was raging in Sierra Leone, and they settled on locating the mission in Bompeh Chiefdom by the coast. For a while Sengbeh maintained contact with the mission but he left to trade along the coast. Little is known of him after that.

A year before Sengeh Pieh returned, a British Admiral, Joseph Denman, commanded a naval expedition up the Gallinas river to rescue a black British subject and her child, He forced the Vai leaders, King Siaka and Prince Manna to sign an agreement banning the slave trade throughout their Gallinas territory. He then burned down the barracoons of the Spanish slave dealers.

1841

At the end of the historic La Amistad case, the U.S. Supreme Court ruled Sengbeh Pieh and others had been illegally forced into slavery, and thus are free under American law.

1849

Margru (Sarah Kinson) who was a child when she was taken aboard the Amistad, returned to study at Ohio's Oberlin College and then went back to Sierra Leone as an evangelical missionary.

Five year later in 1845, a British Commodore burnt down the homes of Prince Manna and his subjects in retribution for the violation of Denman's agreement. The abolition of slavery message was finally received in the Gallinas territory, the last vestige of slavery activities in Sierra Leone.

THE LAST SET OF LIBERATED AFRICAN SET FOOT ASHORE ON FREETOWN IN 1863 BRINGING THE ESTIMATED TOTAL LIBERATED AFRICANS WHO DISEMBARKED SINCE 1808 TO OVER 83,000 AFRICANS. THE BRITISH PARLIAMENT ENACTED THE ACT TO ABOLISH THE SLAVE TRADE IN MARCH 1807. THE BRITISH GOVERNMENT ON NEW YEAR'S DAY 1808 TOOK CONTROL OF FREETOWN FROM THE SIERRA LEONE COMPANY THAT HAD MANAGED THE COLONY FROM ITS FOUNDING. FREETOWN BECAME THE BASE FOR A VICE-ADMIRALTY COURT TO BE SET UP FOR THE TRIAL AND ADJUDICATION OF ANY CAPTURED SLAVE SHIP WITH ENSLAVED AFRICANS. THE COURT'S ROLE WAS TO PROSECUTE THE SLAVERS AND SETTLE THE LIBERATED AFRICANS WITHIN THE COLONY. APPRENTICING LIBERATED AFRICAN TO MEMBERS OF THE EARLIER SETTLER POPULATION WAS THE INITIAL METHOD OF SETTLEMENT AND LATER GROUPS OF LIBERATED AFRICANS WERE SETTLED IN VILLAGES AROUND THE PENINSULA. THE VICE-ADMIRALTY COURT WAS SUSPENDED AFTER A DECADE AND WAS REPLACED BY BILATERAL COURTS OF MIXED COMMISSION IN 1819. THIS INTERNATIONAL COURT OPERATED IN FREETOWN UNTIL IT WAS OFFICIALLY CLOSED IN 1871.

1849

Lighthouse at Cape Sierra Leone was completed and lit on December 31st to bring in the New Year in 1850.

1871

Mary and Joseph Gomer, black missionary couple of United Brethen Mission, arrived in Sierra Leone to set up the mission in Shenge. The were greeted by Sherbro Chief Thomas Caulker.

JOHN
HENRY SMYTHE

1915 - 1996

Lt. John Henry Smythe was born in Freetown on June 30 1915. He attended the Sierra Leone Grammar School and after joining the British Colonial Force in Sierra Leone, he arned the title of Sergeant in 1939 at the age of 24.

During early to mid 20th century, conditions for Africans and blacks in military forces around the world was grim. Desegregation in the US armed forces took place around 1948. Sierra Leone, however had experienced a long history of engaging in foreign military conflicts and enlistment in colonial forces before World War II. A large group of Black Loyalists who had fought on the side of the American Revolutionary War had settled and established the settlement of Freetown in 1787 and 1792. A group of Jamaican Maroons who had fought with and against the British in Jamaica had also settled in Freetown in 1800. Many of the Maroon settlers carried titles such as Captain and Major, illustrating the ranks they were given in their militia.

The West India Regiment was formed in 1795 as a way to enlist blacks and reinforce numbers the British needed for wars in America and the Caribbean. Many Africans liberated from slave ships after the British abolished the trade in 1807, were recruited and enlisted in the West India Regiment and Royal African Corps. The West India Regiment took part in several notable wars, including Napoleonic Wars, the War of 1812 in America, and the Battle of New Orleans in 1815.

1792

Black Loyalists who fought during the American Revolutionary War settled in Freetown, Sierra Leone.

1819

Disbandment of West Indian Regiment in Sierra Leone. Many of them were Afro-West Indians from the Caribbean as well as Liberated Africans freed from captured slave ships.

In 1819 and the 1820s, the West India Regiment was disbanded in Freetown and many of the soldiers settled in places such as Waterloo, Murray Town, and Gloucester. Many of them would later take part in the First Ashanti War of 1824, and other wars along the West African coast. During World War I, Sierra Leoneans in the West India Regiment gained military experience fighting against the Germans in Cameroon.

During World War II, thousands of Africans were recruited by Allied Forces to fight in North Africa, where major battles were taking place against the Germans. In 1944, thousands of French West Africans fought in Italy and Sicily. The British recruited thousands of West Africans from countries such as South Africa, Nigeria, the Gambia, Gold Coast, and Sierra Leone, to join the West African Frontier Force. These forces fought alongside allied forces in Japan and Germany.

"SIERRA LEONEANS IN THE ROYAL WEST AFRICAN FRONTIER FORCE, TOOK PART IN THE BURMA CAMPAIGN DURING WORLD WAR II"

In 1940, John Smythe became a Navigator for the Royal Air Force and joined the 619 Bomber Squadron during World War II, becoming one of Britain's first black airmen. He was one of a few men who completed training as a navigation officer for the Royal Air Force. Several West Africans from Sierra Leone, Nigeria, Gold Coast and other countries volunteered to fight in the global war. Part of John Smythe's motivation for fighting in this war was to help stop Germany's Hitler from gaining global power. For John, Hitler's racist ideology for blacks was another motivation for enlisting.

After flying about 22 missions successfully, in November, 1943 his plane was shot down and he was taken prisoner by German soldiers. After spending several months as a Prisoner of War, he was freed by Russian forces in 1945 and returned to Britain.

After the war, in 1948, John Smythe was placed in charge of coordinating an important period of West Indian immigration into Britain, known as the Windrush. The Windrush era was a monumental one for post-war emigration of West Indians into Britain.

1900

West African Frontier Force was established. The Sierra Leone Battalion became a part of it.

1944

West Africans soldiers enlisted with Allied Forces took part in the taking of Burma in Asia, from the Japanese. Africans who had demonstrated heroism and gallantry were denied the Victoria Cross, British Empire's highest medal.

After World War II, a large group of West Indian emigrants arrived in the United Kingdom on the Empire Windrush ship. The ship included hundreds of airmen from Jamaica, Barbados and other Caribbean countries, who had served in the war. The Windrush generation, which lasted between 1948 and 1971, continues to influence British immigration policy to-date.

John Smythe later studied law, becoming a Barrister in 1951. In 1953, at the coronation of Queen Elizabeth II, he represented the Sierra Leone Naval Volunteer Force. In 1961, he became Solicitor-General of the newly constituted Republic of Sierra Leone. In 1978, he was awarded the Order of the British Empire (OBE).

SIERRA LEONE WAS A VERY ACTIVE PARTICIPANT DURING WORLD WAR II. A WEST AFRICAN WAR COUNCIL MET REGULARLY IN FREETOWN TO SET OUT PLANS OF OPERATION FOR SIERRA LEONE AND OTHER WEST AFRICAN COUNTRIES FOR THE WAR. FREETOWN'S HARBOUR WAS USED REGULARLY TO STATION WAR SHIPS BOUND FOR EUROPE. A NAVAL BASE WAS MAINTAINED IN FREETOWN BY THE BRITISH. OVER 20,000 AFRICANS WERE EMPLOYED TO CONSTRUCT A NAVAL DEFENSE STRUCTURE TO PROTECT THE HARBOUR.

LOCAL NEWSPAPERS, SUCH AS THE DAILY GUARDIAN AND THE AFRICAN STANDARD, PUBLISHED ARTICLES ILLUSTRATING THE OPINIONS OF SIERRA LEONEANS FOR AND AGAINST THE WAR. DRILLS AND SIRENS SOUNDED THROUGHOUT THE CITY, AS OFFICIALS PREPARED THE RESIDENTS. AS WARTIME MENTALITY TOOK OVER FREETOWN, STEPS WERE TAKEN TO DEVELOP THE MINDSET OF RESIDENTS. CHURCHES RANG BELLS ALONG WITH SIRENS, WATER WAS SHUT OFF AT SPECIFIC TIMES, SCHOOLS CLOSED, AND VARIOUS SITES WERE TRANSFORMED INTO WAR-READY FACILITIES.

THE RISE IN MILITARIZED UNIONS HAD MAJOR EFFECTS ON MOBILIZATION EFFORTS. IN 1939, THE WAR DEPARTMENT AMALGAMATED WORKER'S UNION HELD STRIKES AT THREE SITES PREPARING FOR THE WAR.

1945

Japan surrenders, bringing an end to World War II. Germany also surrendered to the Soviets the same year.

1971

Royal Sierra Leone Military Force was renamed the Republic of Sierra Leone Military Force.

DR.LETTIE
STUART

1917 - 2011

Lettie Stuart was born in Freetown, Sierra Leone in 1917. Her paternal ancestor was Melvin Stuart, an Afro-West Indian who arrived in Sierra Leone in the late 1800s to serve as a customs officer. On her mother's side, her grandfather was Canon. C.W. Farquhar who took up a position as Head of the Anglican Church Missionary Society mission to the Isles de Los off Conakry, Guinea in 1890. He came from the Caribbean island of Antigua.

The Farquhars were a family of educationists. Lettie Stuart's grandfather Farquhar had at one time been Master of the Micro Model School in Antigua. Her mother, Amy Stuart, taught French and Music at the Freetown Secondary School for Girls (FSSG) for many years, and her aunt, Olive Conton, was a teacher at the Annie Walsh Memorial School. Her sister, Melvine Stuart, taught for a while at the FSSG and spent the rest of her career with the Ministry of Education. Her cousin, William Conton, became a lecturer at Fourah Bay College and later served as Principal of Accra High School and Bo School. His twin sister Elizabeth also became a teacher.

1814

A Christian Institution was established at Leicester Village to educate boys and girls, most of whom had been rescued from slave ships. This was the forerunner of Fourah Bay College

1861

Annie Walsh Memorial School had about 30 students admitted. It was the first Secondary school for girls in West Africa.

According to an article in the Sierra Leone Studies journal by Dr. Paul E.H. Hair, between 1827 and 1950, a little over 1,000 students had been admitted at the Fourah Bay College. During the 1800s, admission remained standard at around 10 students added each decade. By the 1940s, this had changed significantly, with over 300 admitted that decade alone.

One of the college's first students and its first graduate was Samuel Ajayi Crowther, who later became the first African Bishop ordained by the Anglican Church. Many of the college's first students up to the late 1800s were usually trained to become schoolmasters and missionaries. Many former students such as William Tamba and James Quaker went on to serve as Catechists or Schoolmasters in the Anglican Church Missionary Society in Sierra Leone.

"FOURAH BAY COLLEGE HAS PART OF ITS ORIGIN IN THE CHRISTIAN INSTITUTION ESTABLISHED AT LEICESTER VILLAGE. IN 1815, A TEMPORARY HOUSE FOR BOYS AND ANOTHER FOR GIRLS WERE BUILT. AT THE TIME, THERE WERE 37 BOYS AND 6 GIRLS. IT WASN'T UNTIL 1938 THAT THE FIRST FEMALE, GRADUATED FROM FOURAH BAY COLLEGE"

Fourah Bay College had earned the name, "Athens of West Africa", mainly because of its stellar quality of education and the diversity of its students, from all across the region. By the 1940s, students originated from Nigeria, Ghana, and the Gambia, among other places.

Lettie Stuart attended the FSSG and entered Fourah Bay College as one of its first female students. No female had been admitted into the college leading to graduation, until the 1930s. Five females were admitted during that decade. Lettie Stuart became the second woman to graduate from Fourah Bay College, following Lati Hyde-Forster.

She began her career in the late 1940s as a lecturer at Fourah Bay College and served as Warden of Female Students. In 1956 she became Principal of the FSSG and served in that capacity

1878

Fourah Bay College had become affiliated with Durham University. The first set of degrees were conferred to graduating students.

1888

Mary Sower's School for Girls was established by the UBC Mission in Moyamba for women in the provinces. It later became the Harford School for Girls.

Lettie Stuart promoted the principles of universal education when she served as Principal Education Officer at the Ministry of Education some time in the 1960s. She represented the Government of Sierra Leone at the International Conference on Public Education.

Always an active member of the Young Womens' Christian Association (YWCA) between 1955 and 1957, she served as National President. Afterwards, she took up an appointment at the YWCA's world headquarters in Geneva, Switzerland and spent most of the 1960s outside Sierra Leone. In 1977 she was appointed a Member of the Board of Governors of the YWCA Vocational Institute. She later founded the Sierra Leone Adult Education Association, a non-profit organization aiming to reduce adult illiteracy and promote non-formal education in Sierra Leone. In recognition of her contribution to Education, in 1988 The University of Sierra Leone awarded Lettie Stuart the Doctorate of Civil Laws Honoris Causa.

WHILE THE FIRST SET OF FEMALE GRADUATES AT FOURAH BAY COLLEGE EMERGED IN THE 1930S, WOMEN AND GIRLS FROM SIERRA LEONE HAD EARNED EDUCATIONAL ACHIEVEMENTS MUCH EARLIER AT INSTITUTIONS OF LEARNING IN OTHER COUNTRIES. IN THE 1880S, ADELAIDE CASELY-HAYFORD WAS ONE OF THE FOUNDING STUDENTS OF THE JERSEY LADIES COLLEGE, A SCHOOL ON AN ISLAND NEAR FRANCE. THE FIRST WEST AFRICAN WOMAN TO EARN A COLLEGE DEGREE IN MEDICINE WAS AGNES YEWANDE SAVAGE, BORN IN NIGERIA BUT WITH WITH SIERRA LEONEAN ANCESTRY. SHE EARNED IT IN 1929

1938

Lati Hyde-Forster became the first woman to graduate from Fourah Bay College. Years later she became the first African Principal of the Annie Walsh Memorial School.

1960

Charter establishing Fourah Bay College as the University of Sierra Leone.

ALMAMY
SULUKU
1820s-1906

Alimamy Suluku has been regarded by many as one of the greatest Limba Chiefs of his era. He was the son of Sankailay, a powerful ruler of the Biriwa Limba region. Suluku's brother's name was Bubu and according to Paramount Chief Masa Paki Kebombor II, they descended from a Madingo ancestor who came and settled in the Limba region decades earlier. Legend states that Amadu was his name and Almamy Suluku were titles given to him when he became ruler.

Starting around 1873, he ruled his Biriwa chiefdom for the next 20 years. He dominated the economic, political, and military interests of his people and helped to make Biriwa and nearby towns in the northern region of Sierra Leone a center of power.

During Suluku's era, most Limbas resided in the northern region of Sierra Leone, especially places such as Kabala, Bafodea, Bumban, Karina, and other nearby towns. In the 19th century, the three main Limba regions in Sierra Leone were Bumban, Bafodea and Tonko Limba.

1727
Major conflict in Fuuta Jalon between the Fula and Yalunka. The State of Falaba emerged strongly during this time.

1768
According to Historian Christopher Fyfe, the town of Falaba was built. The previous year, the Solima invaded the Limba and took more than 3,000 to Rio Pongo (Conakry region) for enslavement.

Suluku, based in Bumban, capitalized on the advantage of his town's location along a key trading route to Fuuta Jalon. During his era, Sierra Leone had a thriving trade system that linked Freetown, the provinces, and Guinea. Yalunka, Mende, Krio, Koranko and others were active in trade with each other, and products such as gold, cattle, and cotton flourished.

Traders regularly presented him with gifts, while regional leaders and diplomats honored him with visits and praise throughout his rule. He worked diligently to integrate Madingos into his chiefdom, seeking protection from Samori Toure, a powerful ruler of a West African empire. He also helped to bring an end to the slave trade in his towns.

"ACCORDING TO SIERRA LEONEAN PROFESSOR AND HISTORIAN, JOE A.D. ALLIE, SULUKU WAS A NICKNAME MEANING WOLF. HE WAS VIEWED BY MANY AS VERY SUPERSTITIOUS AND ASSOCIATED WITH MAGIC. HIS LEGENDARY TALES HAVE LONG BEEN INCLUDED IN LIMBA FOLKTALES AND STORIES."

In the 1870s, a major trade route that passed through Kabala was destroyed by Limbas in Yagala. Suluku and the ruler of Kabala created an alliance and created another route that traders could use.

Around the early 1880s, Samori Toure's Sofa troops occupied Biriwa chiefdom. They posed a great threat to the existing economic and political structures established in the Limba region, particularly with threats of the Mandingo. In 1886, Suluku and Alimamy Suman, ruler of the Wara Wara Limba, sent a petition to the British requesting assistance in protecting trade routes. With help from the British, the Sofa troops were driven out.

In the 1880s, Suluku utilized all of his authority, strategy and diplomacy to protect his people from the invading Sofa, Samori Toure's military force. During the Hut Tax War in 1898, Suluku tried his best to remain peaceful, however he supported Bai Bureh by providing with him several resources for his military needs.

1880s

Samori Toure's Sofa warriors attacked Falaba, which led to destruction of the Solima State. Biriwa chiefdom was attacked next and Suluku and others were asked to convert to Islam.

1895

The boundary between Guinea and Sierra Leone is established. In 1897, Kabala became the headquarters of Koinadugu District.

After Suluku's death in 1906, his Biriwa Limba state was divided into Biriwa Limba chiefdom and Saffroko Limba chiefdom. He remains one of the most successful Limba rulers in Sierra Leone history.

Bumban continues to be a prominent place in Limba political history. Many of its leaders have referenced Bumban as a place of influence, either through lineage or training for leadership.

FEATURED IN THE ILLUSTRATION IS CHIEF ALIMAMY SHEKU II, A 20TH CENTURY LIMBA CHIEF OF KAMABIA TOWN, BIRIWA CHIEFDOM, IN BOMBALI DISTRICT. HE LED A DELEGATION PETITIONING FOR A GOVERNMENT SCHOOL IN THE REGION. THIS RESULTED IN THE OPENING OF THE KAMABIA SECONDARY SCHOOL.

1895

One of the four major trade routes in Sierra Leone, identified by the colonial government, runs from Falaba via Bafodia or Koinadugu, through Karene or Bumbun and then to Port Loko.

1915

The Sierra Leone Railway extends from Freetown to Makeni. Surveying for the railway began two decades earlier. The lines ran through parts of western, eastern, and northern regions of the country. The railway closed in 1975.

HARRY
WASHINGTON

1740s - 1800s

A young West African man from around present day Gambia was captured, transported to America and enslaved by George Washington in 1763. He was given the name Harry Washington. George later became America's first president of the United States of America. George offered Harry and three other enslaved Africans as his contribution to the Dismal Swamp project to excavate a canal in the border regions of Virginia and North Carolina. Several years later, Harry was transferred to George Washingon's estate in Mount Vernon, Virginia with his female companion Nan. At the Mount Vernon Plantation, he served as an ostler, tending to horses, and as a house servant until June 1771.

Around the middle of 1775, tensions developed between patriots, those for America's independence and loyalists, those on the side of the British Empire. This led the British Governor of the Virginia colony, Lord Dunmore, to take refuge on a British warship down river from Mount Vernon to mount a defence. From there, he made his famous proclamation that any enslaved person who fights on the side of the British will be freed. So, in July of 1776, when a fleet went up river for fresh water, Harry and others seized the opportunity to run away from George Washington.

In 1779, during the war, Harry was involved in a non-combat role in an army corp of poineers, during the seige of Charleston, which lasted for two months. The British eventually lost the war and they honored their promise to blacks like Harry, who had fought on their side.

1772
The landmark case of James Somerset on June 22, of a freed black man in London whose previous enlsaver attempted to re-enslave him, resulted in the first anti-slavery law in London.

1775
The year King Naimbana's rule of Koya Temne Chiefdom began. He was the overlord of the Bulom shore across the Sierra Leone river.

British troops and over 4,000 freed blacks who were part of the British convoy retreated to New York after the Paris Treaty was signed on November 29, 1782. All blacks who had escaped and fought on the side of the British, were assembled in New york aboard ships to Nova Scotia, Canada. They were known as Black Loyalists. Harry left on the ship L'Abondance in July 1783 with 405 men, women, and children to Nova Scotia, to a place called Birchtown.

The Black Loyalists lived in tents, log cabins, and unfinished cellars until houses could be built. The group in Birchtown lived in pit houses using timber, moss and earth. For the next decade, they strived to obtain land and build communities during harsh Canadian winters. They eventually organized and dispatched a former Black Pioneer, named Thomas Peters, to London to present a report about the unfair treatment they received from the Nova Scotia Governor. Thomas met another African, Olaudah Equiano, who was an acquaintance of William Wilbeforce and other abolitionists. The abolitionists dispatched John Clarkson to inform the Black Loyalists of a plan to resettle them in Sierra Leone with an earlier group called the Black Poor from London. That effort, added to other Church-based initiatives by group leaders such as George Carroll, David Edmunds, David George, and Moses Wilkinson led to an arrangement to resettle a group of nearly 1,200 Black Loyalists in Sierra Leone.

"ONCE AN ENSLAVED AFRICAN IN THE AMERICA'S, HE RETURNED TO AFRICA WHERE HE LIVED FREE AND DIED FREE."

The group made the journey in 15 ships starting on January 15, 1792 from Nova Scotia, arriving in Sierra leone on March 6, 1792. Their first make-shift community space, called Harmony Hall. It was a space to pray and give thanks for the biblical journey from enslavement to freedom. In the ensuing years, the settlers tried to work with the British-owned Sierra Leone company to get land allocation they had been promised since leaving Nova Scotia. They also advocated strongly for self-rule.

Eight years later, after much work on building Freetown, fighting against the quit-rent levy, French invasion, and Temne incursions, the settlers decided to create their own governing body. On September 3, 1800 they established a new constitution, rules of trade, tax policies, and a process of settling disputes.

1787

On June 11th, Granville Town land grant was signed by King Tom and sub-chiefs Pa Bongee and Queen Yamacouba for the resettlement of about 486 Black Poor from London.

1792

On March 11th, Freetown was established by Nova Scotians arriving on 15 Ships. They were nearly 1,200 formerly Black Loyalists from the US war of independence.

On September 25, 1800, the day the Nova Scotian settlers met to prepare for self-governance, the Jamaican Maroon settlers also arrived on ships from Nova Scotia. The meeting of the settlers was interrupted by soldiers of the British company to preemptively stop the declaration. The chaos that ensued descended into a multiple day siege of the leaders at a brook on the eastern part of the city, not far from Washington's farm. The hill on which he had his farm was called Washington hill (eastern side of Tower Hill).

Although Harry was not present at the initial meeting of the settlers, he later visited settler leaders at the location of the seige. The British promised the Maroons, land allocations if they were successful in ending the siege, and they agreed. The actions of the Maroons dealt a crippling blow to the first major pursuit for "self-governance" from British rule in Sierra Leone. Ironically, overtime, the Maroons also experienced similar disappointments over land allocations promised by the British.

On October 10, 1800 Harry and others were tried in a hurriedly organized British military tribunal for "open and provoked rebellion". He and 23 others were banished to the Bullom Shore across the Sierra Leone river from Freetown. Fourteen years after George Washington won America's freedom, Harry and others were not able to fully secure their own. In retrospect, the once enslaved African returned to Africa from where he was born, to live free and die free.

KING NAIMBANA OF KOYA CHIEFDOM RULED SINCE 1775 FROM ROGBANA TOWN UPSTREAM FROM THE LOCATION OF GRANVILLE TOWN ON THE SIERRA LEONE RIVER. HALF MILE FROM GRANVILLE TOWN GOING OUT TO SEA WAS PA DUFFEE'S TOWN, TWO MILES FURTHER WAS KING JIMMY'S AND BEYOND THAT WAS QUEEN YAMACOUBA'S. CAPE POINT WAS NINE MILES. KING JIMMY WAS THE SUCCESSOR OF KING TOM WHO DIED IN 1788. THE TREATY OF AUGUST 22ND 1788 RE-ESTABLISHED GRANVILLE TOWN (THE CORNERSTONE OF THE COLONY). IT WAS WITNESSED WITH MARKS BY KING NAIMBANA AND KING JIMMY; AND SIGNATURES BY PA BONGEE, THREE BRITISH OFFICIALS, AND BENJAMIN ELLIOTT ON BEHALF OF THE BLACK POOR SETTLERS.

1800

On September 3rd, the Nova Scotian settlers ratified the first self-rule constitution in Sierra Leone involving an administration of hundredors and tithingmen to manage law and commerce.

1800

On September 30, about 500 Jamaica Maroons exiled from Trelawny, Jamaica arrived in Freetown from Nova Scotia and were initially settled in Granville Town.

MADAM
YOKO

1840s - 1906

Madam Yoko was born, Soma, around 1849 in Gbo chiefdom, in the southern province in Sierra Leone. She was known to be a very good dancer in her time.

Her father, Njiakundohun, led a large migration of Mendes west into the Sierra Leone interior, to a settlement around Bo. Her second husband, Gbenjei, had been Chief of Taiama in Sierra Leone. His ancestor had founded that chiefdom. Madam Yoko was married for a third time, to Gbanya Lango, ruler of the Kpaa Mende state and nephew to Gbenjei.

In the early 1880s, after the death of Gbanya in 1878, Madam Yoko was installed as Paramount Chief of the Kpaa Mende, with some assistance from the colonial administration. She became widely known as Queen of Senehun. Senehun had been ceded to the Colonial Government in 1825 and reaffirmed by the Caulker Convention of 1881. Senehun boasted a population of about 1,200 to 1,500 in the late 1880s.

In the 1880s, nearby rival chiefs such as Gbanka, who ruled the Temne of Yoni territory, and Kamanda of Buaya were involved in territorial conflicts with Madam Yoko.

1500s
Mani invasions in the Sierra Leone region. According to Historian Arthur Abraham, the Mende may have originated from a group of Mani migrants.

1880s
Pujehun becomes the ruling headquarters of Momoh KaiKai, ruler of Fula and Mende ancestry. After the Hut Tax War, his town became District Headquarters.

Through her clever diplomacy with the British colonial administration, she developed a strong alliance with the administration, who in turn helped her pursue regional interests. Both Gbanka and Kamanda were captured by the British, and sent to exile during a time most favorable for Yoko's interests.

She proved to be a very useful diplomat for the Colonial Administration and other friendly chiefs. In 1889, she helped coordinate a meeting of chiefs in the Yoni region. A general submission of peace was one of the results of this meeting.

"IN 1896, THE BRITISH DECLARED THE INTERIOR OF SIERRA LEONE A PROTECTORATE. IT WAS DIVIDED INTO 5 DISTRICTS: KARENE, RONIETTA, BANDAJUMA, PANGUMA, AND KOINADUGU."

During the Hut Tax War of 1898, Yoko was favourable to the colonials and obedient to paying the tax. She was one of several chiefs who tried to bring a peaceful close to the resistance to it. Her help to the efforts of the colonial Frontier Force, several stationed in her region, was highly regarded by the Colonial Administration. Other chiefs, such as Nancy Tucker of Bagru, Thomas Neale Caulker of Shenge, and Charles Smart of Mahera also paid the Hut Tax with little issue. During the mende uprising, which took place in the midst of the Hut Tax War, Chief Caulker was killed, while Madam Yoko and Madam Tucker escaped near death experiences.

Madam Yoko's town of Senehun was one of the places destroyed during the Hut Tax War, however the size of some of her other ruling towns increased. In 1899, she moved her home to Moyamba, which had recently become the District Headquarters.

Madam Yoko continued to maintain strong alliances with the colonial administration after the war. In 1899, her and Chief Nancy Tucker traveled to Freetown to attend the funeral of the Secretary for Native Affairs, J. C. Ernest Parkes. As long time friends, she had attended his grand wedding in 1893 with 12 of her dancing girls from Senehun.

1908

The death of Madam Humonya's mother, led to her installment as Paramount Chief. Both served as Paramount Chiefs of Nongowa Chiefdom. The ruling headquarter was moved from Largo to Kenema, which then became District headquarters.

1920s

Kisimi Kamara of Bari Chiefdom in Southern Sierra Leone, created a Mende script, based on the language. It was very popular among Mende students during the 1920s and 1930s.

Madam Yoko had a lot of respect throughout her region, particularly among women. She was a powerful member of the Sande society. She maintained a unit where she trained numerous girls in the Kpaa Mende territory. She passed away in 1906, Paramount Chief of Ronietta District.

ACCORDING TO THE CHALMERS REPORT ON THE INSURRECTION IN THE PROTECTORATE OF SIERRA LEONE, THE COLONIAL GOVERNOR, SIR FREDERICK CARDEW CONDUCTED TOURS AROUND THE PROTECTORATE BEFORE THE WAR, OUTLINING INTENDED LAWS TO BE ENACTED IN THE PROTECTORATE. CARDEW HELD MEETINGS IN KARENE, MADINA, KAMBIA, SHENGE AND OTHER TOWNS, WITH REGIONAL CHIEFS TO INFORM THEM. CHALMERS CONCLUDED THAT MANY OF THESE MEETINGS RESULTED IN NO ASSENT BY THE CHIEFS TO THESE NEW LAWS.

CHALMERS ACKNOWLEDGED THAT INSTRUCTIONS ABOUT THE HUT TAX HAD BEEN SENT TO PORT LOKO, SANDA LOKO, KARENE AND OTHER TEMNE TOWNS, THOUGH THERE WERE NO REACTIONS OF APPROVAL MADE BY THE CHIEFS. THE COLONIAL GOVERNOR RECEIVED SEVERAL PETITIONS FROM SEVERAL CHIEFS NOTING THEIR REFUSAL TO PAY THE TAX AND CALLS FOR THE ORDINANCE ENFORCING IT, POSTPONED. ALL OF THESE WERE HOWEVER IGNORED BY THE COLONIAL GOVERNOR WHO, INSTEAD CHOSE TO ENFORCE THE HUT TAX WITH FORCE.

MADAM YOKO SENT A LETTER IN 1896 TO THE COLONIAL GOVERNOR, ACCEPTING THE ORDINANCE, BUT ONLY TENTATIVELY. SHE NOTED THAT IT WAS NEW TO THE PROTECTORATE AND THERE NEEDED TO BE A TRIAL PERIOD TO SEE IF IT WAS INDEED VIABLE FOR THE PEOPLE OF THE PROTECTORATE TO ABIDE BY.

1933

African American Linguist, Dr. Lorenzo Dow Turner, recorded a Mende song by Amelia Dawley in Georgia. The song had been preserved in her Gullah family for over 200 years.

1963

Professor Milton Harvey stated that by 1963, Bo had a population of 26,613 compared to about 3,000 in 1927.

REFERENCES

Abraham, A. (1971). The rise of traditional leadership among the Mende: A study in the acquisition of political power. Dept. of History, Fourah Bay College, University of Sierra Leone.

Abraham, A. (1978a). Cultural policy in Sierra Leone. Unesco.

Abraham, A. (1978b). Mende government and politics under colonial rule: A historical study of political change in Sierra Leone, 1890-1937. Sierra Leone University Press.

Abraham, A., United States, Department of State, & Office of International Information Programs. (1998). The Amistad revolt: An historical legacy of Sierra Leone and the United States. U.S. Dept. of State, International Information Programs.

Alie, J. A. D. (2005). A new history of Sierra Leone. Macmillan.

Arkley, A. S. (1965). Slavery in Sierra Leone.

Bledsoe, C. (1984). The political use of Sande ideology and symbolism. American Ethnologist, 11(3), 455–472.

Campbell, Mavis C. (1990). The Maroons of Jamaica, 1655-1796: A history of resistance, collaboration & betrayal. Africa World.

Campbell, Mavis Christine, & Ross, G. (1993). Back to Africa: George Ross and the Maroons: from Nova Scotia to Sierra Leone. Africa World Press.

Caulker-Burnett, I. (2010). The Caulkers of Sierra Leone: The story of a ruling family and their times. Xlibris.

Chambers, V., & Lee, P. (1998). Amistad rising: A story of freedom. Harcourt Brace.

Childs, G. (2015). The Language Ecology of Sierra Leone. The Journal of Sierra Leone Studies.

Clifford, M. L. (2006). From slavery to Freetown: Black Loyalists after the American Revolution. McFarland.

Coker, E. A. (2016). Reflections on Sierra Leone by a Former Senior Police Officer: The History of the Waning of a Once Progressive West African Country. iUniverse.

Cole, G. R. (2013). The Krio of West Africa: Islam, culture, creolization, and colonialism in the nineteenth century. Ohio University Press.

Cromwell, A. M. (2014). An African Victorian Feminist: The Life and Times of Adelaide Smith Casely Hayford 1848-1960. Taylor and Francis.

Crowder, M. (1970). West African chiefs: Their changing status under colonial rule and independence. Transl. from the French by Brenda Packman. Africana Publ. Corp.

Day, L. (2012). Gender and power in Sierra Leone: Women chiefs of the last two centuries. Palgrave Macmillan.

Fanthorpe, R. (1998). Limba deep rural strategies. Journal of African History., 39, 15–38.

Finnegan, R. H. (1963). The traditional concept of chiefship among the Limba. Sierra Leone Studies., 17, 241–253.

Finnegan, R. H. (1967). Limba stories and story-telling. Clarendon P.
Fishing in rivers of Sierra Leone oral literature. (2001). People's educational Association of Sierra Leone.

Fyfe, C. (1962). A short History of Sierra Leone. Longmans.

Fyfe, C. (1964). Sierra Leone inheritance. Oxford University Press.

Fyfe, C., & Jones, C. (1991). Our children free and happy: Letters from Black settlers in Africa in the 1790s. Edinburgh University Press.

Fyle, C. M., & Foray, C. P. (2006). Historical dictionary of Sierra Leone. Scarecrow Press.
Great Britain, & Central Office of Information. (1961). Sierra Leone [a nation is born].

REFERENCES

Harris, J. M. (1866). Some Remarks on the Origin, Manners, Customs, and Superstitions of the Callinas People of Sierra Leone. Journal of the Anthropological Society of London, 4, lxxxii–lxxxv.

Hoffer, C. P. (1972). Mende and Sherbro women in high office. Canadian Journal of African Studies Canadian Journal of African Studies, 6(2), 151–164.

Jalloh, A. (1999). African entrepreneurship: Muslim Fula merchants in Sierra Leone. Ohio University Center for International Studies.

Jones, A. (1981). Who were the Vai? Journal of African History., 22, 159–178.

Kallon, M. F., Amara, T. M., & Ensa-N'Dayma, F. (2019). The Kissi people of West Africa.

Kup, A. P. (1962). A history of Sierra Leone, 1400-1787: [Reprint. University Press.

Lowther, K. (2012). The African American odyssey of John Kizell a South Carolina slave returns to fight the slave trade in his African homeland. University of South Carolina Press.

M.C.F. Easmon. (1959). Paul Cuffee. Sierra Leone Studies, 12, 196–200

M.C.F. Easmon. (1958). Madam Yoko: Ruler of the Mendi Confederacy. Sierra Leone Studies, 11, 165–168.

Megill, E. L. (2004). Sierra Leone remembered. Author House.

Mitchell, P. K. (1962). Trade routes of the early Sierra Leone Protectorate. Sierra Leone Studies., 16, 204–217.

MORROW, J. H. (2010). Black Africans in World War II: The Soldiers' Stories. The Annals of the American Academy of Political and Social Science, 632, 12–25.

Nicol, D. (1960). West Indians in West Africa. Sierra Leone Studies., 13, 14–23.

Nicol, D. (1967). Africa—A subjective view. Longmans.

Ottenberg, S. (2014). Olayinka: A woman's view: the life of an African modern artist.

Paracka, D. J. (2015). The Athens of West Africa: A history of international education at Fourah Bay College, Freetown, Sierra Leone.

Patton, A. (1996). Physicians, colonial racism, and diaspora in West Africa. University Press of Florida.

Pybus, C. (2006). Washington's Revolution (Harry that is, not George). Atlantic Studies, 3(2), 183–199.

Pybus, C. (2007). Epic journeys of freedom: Runaway slaves of the American Revolution and their global quest for liberty. Beacon Press.

Reeck, D. (1976). Deep Mende: Religious interactions in a changing African rural society. E.J. Brill.

Reed, T., & Robinson, J. A. (2016). The Chiefdoms of Sierra Leone

Scotland, D. W. (1955). Notes on Bai Bureh, of 1898 fame. Sierra Leone Studies: The Journal of the Sierra Leone Society Sierra Leone Studies, 5, 11–19.

Skinner, D. E. (1976). Islam and Education in the Colony and Hinterland of Sierra Leone (1750-1914).

Canadian Journal of African Studies / Revue Canadienne des Études Africaines Canadian Journal of African Studies / Revue Canadienne des Études Africaines, 10(3), 499.

Thomas, L. D. (1986). Rise to be a people: A biography of Paul Cuffe. Univ. Press of Chicago.

Turshen, M., & Holcomb, B. (1993). Women's lives and public policy: The international experience. Greenwood Press.

Tylden, G. (1962). THE WEST INDIA REGIMENTS, 1795 to 1927, and from 1958. Journal of the Society for Army Historical Research, 40(161), 42–49.

Walker, J. W. St. G. (2019). The Black Loyalists: The Search for a Promised Land in Nova Scotia and Sierra Leone, 1783-1870.

Wyse, A. (2002). H.C. Bankole-Bright and politics in colonial Sierra Leone, 1919-1958. Cambridge University Press.

ABOUT THE AUTHORS

AKINDELE T.M. DECKER

Akindele Decker is a poet and writer born in Sierra Leone, West Africa. His first breakthrough in poetry was at the age of 15, with his first published Poem, 'What If' in 1998. His poems cover topics dealing with the middle-passage, identity, and African history. In 2004, Akindele received an Editors Choice Award for outstanding achievement in Poetry from the International Library of Poetry. He conducted poetry workshops for Secondary School students in Croydon, England in 2005. In 2012, he performed "Dancing in Blue Waters" at Busboy & Poets in Washington D.C., chronicling the middle-passage of the Trans-Atlantic Slave trade. One of his most recent work was in 2016 with GWB Commission's ONE Campaign, celebrating the diverse ancestral heritage of Sierra Leoneans. He has served as a panelist and presenter for several platforms including the American Association of State and Local History on the topic of intercultural identity; and Prince George's African American Museum and Cultural Center on Maroon culture and the global African Diaspora. He resides in Maryland, USA with his family.

ADRIAN Q. LABOR

Adrian Q. Labor extended his interest for everything Sierra Leonean by taking up two new hobbies over time alongside his current profession as a Civil Engineer. His first hobby focused on building an online genealogy of the founding settlers of the city of Freetown. He then followed up with a second one to conduct literature research on the Icons of Sierra Leone who shaped the country's diverse national and rich international history. Through the insights gained, he was drawn to the opportunity to create this illustrated history book series. Out of this labor of love, Adrian began a family tradition to share an article at the end of the year to his extended family in which he recounts historic connections and highlights contributions of paternal and maternal ancestors. His most recent article was about events in the 1790s that led to the establishment of Freetown. The title was "Last Christmas in Nova Scotia, America and their Hopes of Better and Brighter New Year in Sierra Leone, Africa." This first book, "20 Icons of Sierra Leone Who Shaped History", which he co-authors, remakes historic connections and highlights contributions of national ancestors of all young adults of Sierra Leonean parentage.

SAMANTHA EVERETTE

Samantha Everette has dedicated her life and career to art and design. She is an award winner footwear designer with over 10 years of industry experience. Samantha is a passionate photographer and illustrator. She is committed to capturing and boasting the beauty of Black people through her art and photography.